TRICKS TWISTS

Andre
KOLE
and Jerry
MacGREGOR

HARVEST HOUSE PUBLISHERS
Eugene, Oregon 97402

Cover design by Terry Dugan Design, Minneapolis, Minnesota
Illustrations by Joneile Emory

Tricks and Twists
Copyright © 1998 by André Kole and Jerry MacGregor
Published by Harvest House Publishers
Eugene, Oregon 97402

Library of Congress Cataloging-in-Publication Data
Kole, André.
    Tricks and twists / André Kole and Jerry MacGregor.
        p.   cm.
    ISBN 1-56507-974-4
    1. Magic tricks.   I. MacGregor, Jerry.   II. Title.
GV1547.K65 1998
793.8--dc21   98-15499
                                                                CIP

Printed in the United States of America.

98 99 00 01 02 03 / BP / 10 9 8 7 6 5 4 3 2 1

Dedication

To my two grand little illusionists
Dustin Kole and Dillon Kyle
with love from Papa K.

For Kaitlin Victoria MacGregor
with all my love
—Papa

Contents

The World of Illusion

The World of Illusion

Magic. From simple tricks done around a campfire to elaborate shows performed in castles, people have been fascinated by it for centuries. In ancient times it was often associated with religion, but there is nothing supernatural about magic tricks—they are *illusions*, entertaining tricks that twist the facts and fool the eyes.

As we head into the twenty-first century, we are surrounded by some of the most amazing magic tricks ever: Men walk on the moon, special cameras see inside our bodies, and images travel through the air to be seen on our television sets. Yet people are still fascinated with the same simple tricks that fooled others centuries ago: coins that disappear, rings that link together, and scarves that appear from nowhere. Since we love illusions, this book is our way of sharing some of our favorites with you.

For more than 30 years, André Kole has been fooling and entertaining people with his *World of Illusion*, a spectacular show that has been seen in 76 countries around the globe. In fact, André has performed in more countries throughout the world than any other magician in history! His performances, done in cooperation with Campus Crusade for Christ, have given André a wonderful opportunity not only to entertain but to share the story of his spiritual journey with millions of people.

Jerry MacGregor, who shares André's love of illusion, is a full-time writer who has been practicing and performing magic tricks since he was nine years old—and now he wants others to enjoy the fun. You'll find the illusions in this book enjoyable, simple to do, and inexpensive to create. They can be performed with everyday objects you'll find around your home: pencils and paper clips, spoons and scarves. Most importantly, they provide a wonderful way to entertain yourself and others. So dive in and discover how much fun you can have with *Tricks and Twists!*

André Kole
Jerry MacGregor

1

Quick Tricks and Easy Illusions

The Secret of Success

 ——————————

At the start of each chapter, we'll share with you one of the "secrets" we've found that have helped make us better illusionists. The first and most important secret is very simple: *Practice!* Without practice, your tricks won't fool people. Rarely can we read something in a book and immediately perform it well. So *practice your tricks*, and soon you'll be fooling everyone!

André Kole's Knot Disintegrator

In the movies, the hero will sometimes use a "time machine" to go back in time and correct a mistake. In this trick, you'll create your own miniature time machine—and all it requires is 1 cardboard toilet-paper tube and 1 piece of rope 2 feet long.

The Trick: The trickster (that's you!) ties a loose knot in a piece of rope and tells this story: *"I've always wanted to know what it would be like to travel backward in time. After months of research, I finally created my own time machine."* Hold up the cardboard tube, with the words "Time Machine" printed on it. *"Everything that goes inside the time machine goes backward in time one minute. For example, one minute ago there was no knot in this rope. If I pass the knotted rope through the time machine, you'll see that it instantly changes back to the way it was one minute ago—unknotted!"* With those words you drop the knot into the time machine, and when you pull it out, the knot has vanished!

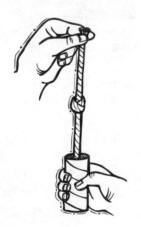   

Figure 1   Figure 2

The Twist: To accomplish this trick, simply cut a hole about the size of a quarter in the tube. Keeping the hole turned away from your audience, secretly stick your index finger through it and into the knot. That way, as you gently pull the rope out, the knot will unwind around your finger. Miracle accomplished!

Figure 3

Linking Paper Clips

One of the oldest tricks in magic is called the "linking rings," in which solid metal rings pass through each other, defying the laws of science. Here is a simple way to duplicate that famous trick.

Here's What Happens: Fold a dollar bill in thirds. Place one paper clip around the first and second folds. Place the other clip around the second and third folds, as in the illustration. Pull the upper corners away from each other in one quick motion and the paper clips will fly off the bill *magically linked together!*

Remember: Good performances require preparation. Practice this trick at home until you get the knack.

The Balancing Wand

In this trick, you'll show everyone how to defy gravity!

Getting Ready: Cut a strip of black paper ten inches long and two inches wide, then roll it into a circle the short way so it resembles a magic wand. Tape it together, and put 2 small round lead fishing weights inside. (If they are too large, pound them flat with a hammer.) Next, cut two pieces of white construction paper for the wand's tips. Neatly close and tape them on the ends.

Performing the Trick: Ask your audience, *"Have you ever wanted to travel in space? I've always wanted to see what it felt like to live in a world without gravity."* Then pick up the wand as you say, *"For example, this wand was brought back from space, and it is immune to gravity. Let me explain. Like all wands, it can balance in the middle."* Make sure the weights are in the center of the wand, and balance it on your finger. *"However, since this wand is from outer space, it can also balance on one end."* Swing the wand in a gentle circle, causing the weights to slide toward one end of the wand, then place the weighted end on the edge of a table, causing the wand to stick straight out. Now say, *"Of course, if you don't understand science, you won't be able to make the wand work,"* as you place it on someone's finger with the weighted end away from them. The weights will cause the wand to fall down. *"However, since I understand the scientific principles, I can cause the wand to defy gravity!"* Place the wand on the fingertips of both hands, then slowly move one hand away. The weighted end will allow the wand to rest on one finger, magically sticking straight out from your finger.

The Floating Pencil

By pretending to use your "static electricity," you can make a pencil rise up and down—even when you are far away from it!

You will need: 1 sharp pencil; 1 empty pop bottle; a small black thread; 2 dabs of soft wax.

The Trick: Place the bottle on the table, drop the pencil inside, and ask, *"Have you noticed how much static electricity is in the air lately? My body has been full of it, and you know how electricity attracts metal."* Rub your right index finger against your chest for a few seconds, then hold it over the mouth of the bottle as you say, *"For example, watch what happens when I rub my finger and try to attract the lead in this pencil."* The pencil will begin to mysteriously rise out of the bottle as you say, *"With this much static electricity, I'm thinking of going to work for the electric company!"*

The Twist: Rub the wax between your fingers for a minute to soften it, press the ends of the thread into it, then place one dab of wax on your shirt button and the other on the pencil eraser. Place the bottle on the table, insert the pencil with the eraser down, and pretend your finger causes the pencil to rise. Actually, you just have to move your body backwards a bit to make it slowly rise in the bottle. Your audience will look at your finger for an explanation, but the secret is the thread attached to your button. If you smile and act surprised yourself, you're sure to fool them.

The Holdup

The trickster announces, *"One time a magician was walking home late at night, when suddenly he was attacked by a thief who demanded his valuables. The magician had no money on him, only an empty paper bag and a solid gold pen— a magic pen that had been in his family for years. The thief grabbed the pen, put it into a cloth purse, and disappeared into the night. When he got several blocks away, the thief stopped to examine his ill-gotten gains and was surprised to discover the purse was empty! It really had been a magic pen!"* With that the trickster shakes open the handkerchief to show that it is empty. He concludes, *"The magician had somehow transported the pen from the thief's purse back to his own paper bag."* The pen is then produced from the previously-empty bag.

Here's What Happens: All you'll need to do this trick is a handkerchief, a paper bag, and a pen. Place the handkerchief flat on the table (figure 1), fold the bottom up to the top (figure 2), then fold the right half over onto the left to form an impromptu "purse" (figure 3). Grasp this purse by the upper corners with the left hand, and you'll find that it is open on the left side. If you stick a pen into the purse with your right hand (figure 4), you'll find it is easy to secretly slip the pen into your left sleeve—this action is well covered by the handkerchief! When you tell the story of the thief finding his purse empty, simply give the handkerchief a shake with your right hand, proving it empty, then reach into the paper bag with your left hand, letting the pen fall out of your sleeve and into the bag.

Remember: Practicing in front of a mirror will help you see how to slide the pen into your sleeve without anyone noticing. Try it facing different ways, to see which position creates the most cover and stand that way when performing the trick for your audience. You can even pretend to search for the pen, act puzzled, then reach into the bag and act completely surprised to find the pen back where it belongs!

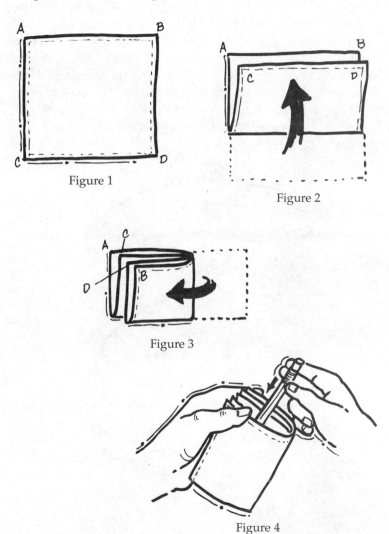

Figure 1

Figure 2

Figure 3

Figure 4

Banana Splits!

Tell a friend you've discovered a way to create banana splits using magic. Hand him a banana, wave your hand over it, and when he opens it, he'll find the banana is already cut in two! How? It's easy: Simply thread a couple feet of silk thread on a long needle, poke it into the banana at one end, pull the thread through, then insert the needle back into the same hole. Go back and forth and few times the length of the banana. When you've got the thread from one end to the other, grasp both ends of the thread and pull firmly, then remove the string. The banana will now be secretly sliced in half— *inside its own peel!*

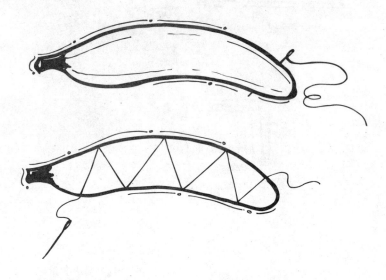

Rising Ring

The famous "Indian Rope Trick" has fascinated people for centuries. Now you can do your own version of that same trick.

You will need: 1 finger ring; 1 pencil; 1 string from an old nylon

The Trick: Begin by telling your audience, *"In the Far East, people have long told stories of Indian fakirs causing a rope to rise magically into the air. The illusionist would play a horn, swaying back and forth, causing the rope to rise like a snake rising from a basket. Let me show you how it was done."* Drop an ordinary finger ring onto a pencil or magic wand, and as you point to it, loudly proclaim, *"Rise! Rise in the air!"* At your command the ring mysteriously rises and falls.

The Twist: The ring is connected to an almost invisible string, which allows you to be able to make it rise and fall on the pencil. To get your string, simply ask your mom for an old nylon stocking, then carefully pull out one of the threads. Tie one end to the ring, the other to a button on your shirt. Place the ring over the pencil in your left hand. To make the ring rise, simply move the end of the wand away from your body. Do this slowly, so people don't notice your hand movement, and it will create a most eerie effect.

Snap Knot

With this trick you apparently make a knot appear in a rope merely by snapping your fingers! Display a rope in your left hand as you say, *"Most people like to hang around magicians."* Take the rope in your right hand and explain, *"For example, sailors love taking magicians sailing with them, because they are able to tie knots with a snap of the fingers!"* With a quick snap, a knot appears in the rope.

Here's What Happens: Using a soft cotton rope or clothesline about three feet long, tie a knot three inches from one end. Display the rope in your left hand, *hiding the knot in your left palm.* Reach over with your right hand, grasp the knot, and pull the entire rope through your left hand, making it appear as though you've fairly shown the entire rope (now the knot is hidden in your *right* hand). Reach down with your left hand and take hold of the dangling end, bring it up to your right hand, so that your right hand

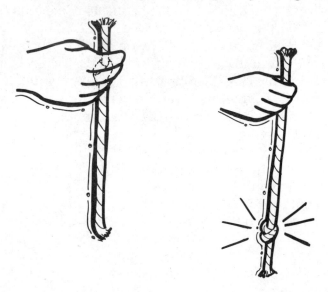

holds both ends of the rope, with the ends sticking out of your right fist. While snapping the fingers of your left hand, drop the knot from your right. It will appear as though you've snapped a knot into the end of the rope!

Remember: People are quick to notice when an illusionist moves too fast. Don't be in a hurry to grab the rope, or to pull it through your hand. Do it carefully, pretending there is no knot to hide, and you're much more likely to fool everyone.

The Houdini Ring

"Houdini is known as the greatest escape artist of all time," the trickster announces. *"But what many people today don't know is that Houdini wasn't just famous for breaking out of jails—he also had the ability to break into them!"* With that, the magician holds up a short piece of rope, stretches it between his hands, and says, *"Pretend this rope is a secure jail. Examine it, and you'll find no breaks, secrets, or trap doors."* The trickster then asks someone to tie the ends of the rope around each wrist, creating *"a circle with my arms—impossible to enter without breaking the circle."* Gesturing to a bracelet on the table, he continues, *"That*

bracelet on the table is no ordinary ring. It is a Houdini ring, capable of incredible feats." Ask for the ring, take it in one hand and ask someone to cover your hands with a large handkerchief or pillowcase. *"Like the magician, the Houdini ring will find a way to break into the jail...and to magically link itself onto the rope!"* With that, the trickster throws off the handkerchief, revealing that the ring has somehow linked itself onto the rope!

The Secret: Two bracelets exactly alike are used. Have the duplicate bracelet pushed over your right hand and concealed in your sleeve before the trick begins. After your hands are tied together and the handkerchief thrown over them, it is a simple matter to pull the concealed bracelet over your hand and onto the rope, and slip the extra bracelet into your shirt pocket. When you toss off the handkerchief, it will appear as though the bracelet somehow found its way onto the rope—an impossible feat!

Keep in Mind: Tricks are only fun and amusing when they fool us. As soon as you know how a trick is done, it loses its "magic." So don't tell the secrets—it will only spoil it for others.

Quick Tricks

The Tricky Lasso: Hold a stiff cloth napkin in your left hand, the top of the napkin sticking up, then pretend to lasso it with an imaginary lariat in your right hand. As you pull the lariat toward you, the handkerchief bends backward, as though a line was really attached to it. How is it done? Simple: Stick your left thumb into the top of the napkin, secretly moving it to the motions of the lariat. With a bit of practice, you'll soon be able to invisibly move the napkin in any direction!

Solid Thru Solid: Hand a spectator two large safety pins and tell him to link them together. Take them back, and hold one with the opening up and the other with the opening down. Magically pull them apart with a crisp, hard pull. It looks as though steel has penetrated steel, but actually one pin simply slips off the other.

Straight Through: Hold a big safety pin between your thumb and middle finger. Take a wooden stick in your other hand and appear to whip it right through the safety pin. Of course, the stick actually goes *around* the metal pin, but if done quickly, it appears as though the wood penetrates straight through the metal.

Relit: Light a candle and then blow it out. Re-light it *without ever touching a flame to it.* How? Hold a lit match over the candle, and the flame will actually travel down the smoke, re-lighting the candle!

The Broken and Restored Match: Place a wooden match in the center of a handkerchief, fold the handkerchief over it, and have someone break the match.

When you unfold the handkerchief, the match is restored! How do you do it? Place a duplicate match *in the hem of the handkerchief.* That's the one you have the spectator break.

Faster Than You: Challenge a friend to see who can empty a bottle the fastest. You'll always win if you hold the bottle upside-down and rapidly twirl it around in a circular direction. The motion forces the water to the sides, forming a column through which air enters the bottle, and causes the water to escape rapidly.

Mysterious Matchbox: A small matchbox will mysteriously rise on the back of your hand if you catch a fold of skin between the drawer and the cover as you close it. When you bend your hand, the matchbox will stand up on end!

2

Illusions with Everyday Objects

The Secret of Success

 ————————————

Everyone loves a good story, so don't just go through the motions—think of a story to tell as you perform each trick. For example, if you're doing a trick with ropes, perhaps you could tell a story about a trickster on board a sailboat, who could magically make knots appear. A good story turns a simple trick into a minor miracle!

The Rings of Saturn

"*I've been studying astronomy in school,*" the trickster announces, "*and I discovered something fascinating about the mysterious rings surrounding Saturn. For one thing, they don't act like rings on Earth. Here, let me show you.*" The performer holds up a ring made from newspaper. "*This is what rings on Earth look like, and if I cut it in half, I'll get two rings.*" With that the performer gently cuts the ring in half the long way, ending up with two large paper rings.

"*On Saturn, however, the rings seem to be connected in some special way. So if I cut a ring of Saturn, something amazing happens—I get two rings that are linked!*" While saying these words, the performer finds that by cutting a second ring, it turns into two linked rings.

"*And that isn't as strange as the rings of Jupiter. Because it is a much larger planet, if I cut a ring from Jupiter, I get...one giant ring!*" The trickster cuts a third ring, which magically transforms into one large ring.

The Secret: This is a great trick, and it's as easy as can be. Cut four long strips from a newspaper, about two inches wide and as long as you can make them. The secret is in the way each ring is created. For the first ring, simply make a loop and tape the ends together. For the second ring, twist one end completely around two times before taping the ends together. To create the third ring, give one end a half turn, then tape it together. The magic will happen automatically—all you have to do is cut them!

Figure 1   Figure 2   Figure 3   Figure 4

Escapo!

You will need: a matchbox; long ribbon; handkerchief; soft wax

The Trick: The trickster threads a matchbox on a piece of ribbon, asking spectators to hold the ends as he says, *"A poor boy in love with a princess was imprisoned in a dungeon and tied securely with cords."* Next, he throws a handkerchief over the box and reaches underneath with one hand while stating, *"But that poor boy was secretly a magician, and as darkness fell, he slipped out of the cords and escaped the dungeon."* Remove the box while the ribbon is still firmly held in place by the spectators as you say, *"Proving that true love conquers all."*

The Twist: To create *Escapo*, cut apart a matchbox and carefully stick it back together with a dab of soft, sticky wax. It will look completely normal, but will allow you to fool people! Display the matchbox, thread the ribbon through it, and ask two spectators to hold the ends. Show an empty handkerchief, throw it over the matchbox, then (standing to the side so as not to block the audience's view), reach under the handkerchief, unfasten the box, slip it off the ribbon, and quickly stick it back together again before bringing it out from under the handkerchief. With a bit of practice, you'll be doing this with one hand in no time.

Snap and Jump

Place a rubber band around the base of the index and middle fingers of your left hand as you say, *"One thing I learned from André Kole: the hand really is quicker than the eye."* Close your hand into a fist, and use your right hand to pull the rubber band down, stretching it so that the tips of all four left hand fingers are inside the rubber band. It will look like the rubber band is just stretched over two fingers. Hold your hand in a fist, the palm facing the floor, then snap the fingers of your right hand as you say, *"Watch how fast my fingers move."* As you say these words, open your left hand, and the rubber band will appear to jump from the first two fingers to the last two!

In the Dark

Here is a rubber band trick you can perform on a moment's notice.

The Trick: Grab a rubber band in your right hand, then ask a friend to grasp your left fingertip. Say to her, *"I learned a great new trick with this rubber band, but I can only do it in the dark, so let's both close our eyes."* You do, and when you both open them a moment later, the rubber band is hanging from the finger your friend was holding!

The Twist: All you need to perform this mystery are a few identical rubber bands and a long-sleeved shirt. Place a rubber band over your left hand, and hide it under your sleeve. Hold up another rubber band in your right hand. When you both close your eyes, simply stuff the rubber band in your right hand back into your pocket and pull the hidden one into view. When you both open your eyes, the band will somehow have jumped onto your finger, even though the spectator was holding onto that hand.

Remember: You can do this trick in reverse, making the band jump from your left finger back to your right hand by silently sliding the band around your hand back into your left sleeve and pulling the other rubber band from your pocket. But be careful—the second time your spectator knows what to expect and might open her eyes!

Sawing a Lady in Half

You've seen it before: The great magician walks out on stage, cuts the lady in half, then somehow makes her whole again. You can do a very similar trick, using a string, a straw, and some scissors.

Here's What Happens: The magician openly threads a string through an ordinary drinking straw as he says, *"I have practiced sawing a lady in half with six...make that twelve partners. So far I've never been able to get it right! You know how it works—a beautiful lady comes out and slides carefully into a fancy box. Pretend this string is a lady, and this straw the box."* Handing a pair of scissors to a spectator, the magician continues, *"The lady is then cut in half. If you would, please, cut our lady into two pieces."* The magician bends the straw in half and has the spectator snip the top of the straw off. *"But with a wave of the hand, the lady is back together again."* With that, the magician pulls the string out from the straw, instantly restored.

The Secret: Use a razor blade to cut a two-inch-long slit in the center of a straw (figure 1). Have a number of drinking straws in a glass on your table, and casually select the cut straw. Thread a length of string through it as you talk. A wide straw and a fairly stiff piece of string make this much easier. Now as you bend the straw in half, pull down gently on the string, bringing the middle of the string out through the slit in the straw (see figure 2). Conceal this part of the string with your thumb as the spectator cuts off the top of the straw. Push the ends of the straw together, wave your hand over it, remove the string and show it restored.

Figure 1

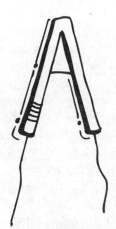

Figure 2

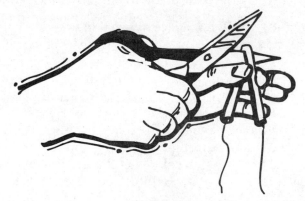

Figure 3

Blind Man's Bluff

Here's one to fool your parents! In this trick, three different-colored cookies are handed to your mom or dad. One is selected and given to you to hold behind your back, then you immediately reveal what color it is—without ever looking at it.

Getting Ready: To prepare for this trick, you need to create three different-colored "cookies" out of red, blue, and green Play-Doh. Press them into a jar lid so that they appear to be *exactly* the same except for color. Next, push a sharp pencil into the middle of each cookie. Make the hole in the red cookie just big enough for a string to be pushed through, the hole in the blue cookie a bit bigger, and the hole in the green cookie even bigger. Don't make the different sized holes too obvious, just enough so that a sharpened pencil will go slightly further into each cookie. Now all you have to do is remember that a pencil will barely go through *red* (the shortest word), will stick out a bit on *blue* (the middle-sized word), and will stick out the farthest on *green* (the longest word).

Performing the Trick: Place a pencil in your back pocket and you're ready to go. Hand the cookies to your mom, saying, *"Practicing all these tricks has made my fingers so sensitive, I can tell colors without even looking!"* Then close your eyes and ask her to select one cookie and place it in your hands behind your back. As soon as you have it, reach into your pocket, grab the pencil, and push it through the center. You'll immediately be able to tell which color was chosen. Pretend to concentrate, and say something like, *"I get a picture of a fire truck. You must have selected red,"* or *"I can tell you're thinking about the ocean, so you must have selected blue."* You can even repeat the trick if you want to!

The Magic Flute

This is Jerry MacGregor's favorite trick for kids. He makes several simple flutes from paper, then allows children to hand him any one they choose. For some reason, Jerry's flute always produces a loud noise, but the kids' flutes never work! Then, to make it even crazier, every time Jerry whispers a magic word into a child's ear, that child is instantly able to make a loud noise on his flute. As the secret is passed around, more and more kids are able to create noises with their flutes.

The Secret: Make a flute from a large square of paper by placing a pencil at the bottom corner of the paper and rolling the paper up diagonally. Put tape around the middle to keep the flute from unraveling. Remove the pencil from inside, and cut the flute three-quarters of the way around the top. The result will be that you've created a reed. Fold the top down flat over the flute in order for it to work properly. The real secret to making a loud noise is that you don't blow into the flute—you inhale! If you blow into it, nothing will happen. But if you inhale it will produce a surprisingly loud sound. Make several flutes, trimming the ends opposite the reeds to different lengths, and each flute will emit a different pitch. (Jerry likes to twiddle his fingers on his flute, as though he were playing notes. The children imitate him, thinking it's the secret to producing sounds.) Try to make it look as if you are blowing into the tube rather than inhaling.

Keep in Mind: Nobody wants to feel stupid, so if someone becomes frustrated with his flute, whisper into his ear, *"The secret is to inhale—but don't tell anyone!"* That way you'll soon have several people joining you in your little band of flutes.

Figure 1

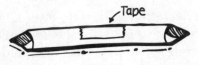

Figure 2

Figure 3

Figure 4

Figure 5

Clean Through

A famous magician in the 1930s, Emil Jarrow, used to amaze audiences by gouging a knife through a handkerchief, then revealing the handkerchief was completely unharmed. You can do a similar trick.

You will need: a coat, a 12-inch square piece of newspaper; a 3-inch pencil

The Trick: A coat is stretched out flat and held by two spectators. A square of newspaper is placed over the center of the coat, and the pencil is made to penetrate clean through it. Although the newspaper is torn in the process, the coat is not harmed!

The Twist: Start by borrowing a coat and saying, *"It's remarkable how well made clothes are these days. For example, look at this coat. Not only is it nice looking, it is almost indestructible."* Ask two spectators to assist you in holding the coat outstretched between their hands at about waist level. Hold the pencil in your right hand, the square of newspaper in your left. Reach underneath the coat with your right hand and gently poke the middle of the coat with the pencil once or twice, so the spectators can see the movement. Place the newspaper in the middle of the coat with your left hand, and pretend to push hard against the pencil underneath, *but don't really push at all.* Act surprised that the pencil didn't come through, pull both hands to the edge of the coat, and bend over as though inspecting the coat. *"You see? All that pushing and nothing happened."* As you say these words, secretly transfer the pencil from your right to your left hand under cover of the newspaper, which you pick up from the coat. Again move your right hand to the center of the coat, poke up once or twice with your finger as you say, *"Here's the pencil."* Then again move the newspaper to the center of the coat with your left hand (the pencil is secretly hidden underneath the newspaper). Now all you must do is grab the pencil through the coat with your right hand as you push it firmly through the newspaper, exclaiming, *"Perhaps if I push extremely hard...ah! There we go!"* Now show that while the paper has a hole in it, the coat is unharmed. *"If only they'd make jeans that wore this well!"*

3

Paper Capers

The Secret of Success

Before you do a trick and tell a story, practice what you are going to say out loud. Stories you've thought through in your mind always sound different when you say them! Don't feel you have to memorize the stories, however, since that can make them sound dull.

Snip-n-Clip

If you often perform tricks for friends, it's nice to have on hand one or two that can be used as a change-of-pace. The tricks in this chapter are all constructed from paper so they are lightweight and easy to handle.

You will need: newspaper; scissors; rubber cement

The Trick: The magician exhibits a strip of newspaper about one inch wide and 14 inches long. *"My little brother is jealous of all the tricks I've been learning, so last night he slipped into my room and found the instructions for my favorite trick."* Fold the strip in half lengthwise and clearly cut it in two as you state, *"Just to bug me, he grabbed a pair of scissors and tried to cut them up. But you know what happened? Nothing! After all, these are tricky instructions."* When you open the strip of paper, it is restored.

The Twist: Cut a sheet of newspaper into strips about one inch wide. Brush the center area of the strip with rubber cement and allow it to dry. To perform the trick, simply show the strip, fold it in half, and cut across the folded end. Let the snipped piece fall to the floor. The strip will be automatically restored thanks to the secret application of rubber cement. When you open it up, the two pieces will cling together, so it looks like you're still holding one long strip of paper. If you want, you can cut the same strip again and again!

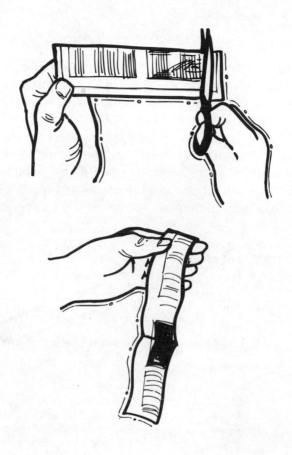

The Paper Tree

The magician displays a roll of newspaper, inserts a forefinger into the center of the roll, and pulls the inside of the tube out to magically form a tree. To perform this very easy trick, roll a sheet of newspaper (the Sunday comics look best!) into a tube, glue a second sheet onto the first using a glue stick, and repeat until you have rolled three or four sheets together. Pick up the tube and cut the top of the tube in four places as illustrated. Then reach in, grab a corner in the center of the tube, and start pulling!

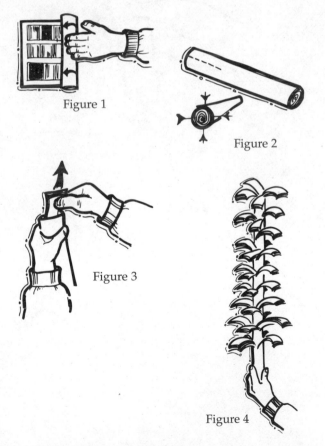

Figure 1

Figure 2

Figure 3

Figure 4

The Transporter

"I'm a big fan of Star Trek," the trickster announces to her friends. *"You know what the best part of that show is? The transporter! Imagine being able to transport something from here to there in an instant. As a matter of fact, I've been able to make my own transporter."* With that, she opens a paper napkin, cuts a 2-inch hole in the center, and slips it around the table leg by gently lifting the table and guiding it through the hole in the center of the napkin. *"Clearly the napkin can't be removed from the table leg without first lifting the table from the floor or tearing the napkin. But I'll do it with my transporter."* She now places the cut out portion of the napkin onto the table, announcing it as her *"transporter control."* Everyone sits at the table, places their hands on the tabletop, and closes their eyes. Making *"transporter"* sounds, the trickster suddenly slaps the control button, then shows everyone that the napkin has transported itself to a different table leg!

The Secret: There are really two napkins. To prepare, tear a hole in the center of one napkin and slip it up onto a table leg. Push it all the way up to the top, hiding it under the tabletop. Be careful to do this without tearing the napkin. When the time is right, start talking about transporters, tear a hole in the second napkin, and openly slide it onto another table leg. Move the napkin up to where you can easily grab it, have everyone sit around the table, and point out the impossibility of removing the napkin without tearing it. Then ask them to close their eyes—but as they do, wet your finger and transfer the moisture to the napkin, allowing you to tear it from the table leg silently. Fold this napkin and put it in your pocket, then gently pull the duplicate napkin down from its hiding place. It will appear as though you've "transported" it from one leg to another!

*What Do You Know?** *

"Sometimes it's awfully hard to tell the truth from a lie," the magician declares as he folds a square of paper. *"Everybody gets fooled sometimes, that's why we've got to look carefully if we want to find the truth. For example,"* he says, cutting the paper with scissors, *"if I cut this paper on both corners, how many holes would you expect to find?"* Opening the sheet, the spectators are surprised to find only one hole!

The Trick: Fold a square piece of paper in half four times as shown. Do it slowly, so your spectators can observe each fold. Then use scissors to cut off the upper right corner. Ask the spectator how many holes the paper will have when it is unfolded. Most people think the answer is four, but when you unfold it, you'll find only one hole.

The Twist: You can also try another trick. Slowly refold the paper along the original creases, then cut the left corner. Ask how many additional holes will be in the paper. *"What do you know,"* you say, *"the answer is none!"*

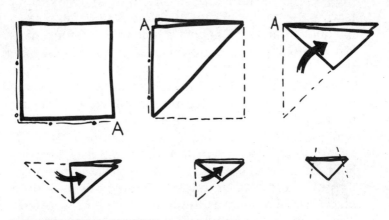

---

* This trick was originally created by J.C. Coy.

Boys vs. Girls*

The trickster says to a girl, *"Would you say boys are a bit strange? Maybe that's why girls don't often want to play with them on the playground. Do me a favor, write the names of some boys you know in the odd-numbered squares on this piece of paper. Then write the names of the girls you know in the even-numbered squares. Now please fold up the piece of paper any way you want, just make sure to use the creases that are already there."* Taking it back, the magician cuts off all four sides of the packet with scissors, hands it to the girl, and asks her to deal the squares onto the table. *"Well look at that! Just like on the playground, the boys and girls are separated."* As the spectators look at the pieces, they find all the girls names are face up, and all the boys names face down.

The Secret: Get a piece of standard typewriter paper and fold it twice each way. When the paper is opened, it will contain 16 squares. Number the squares 1-2-3-4 from left to right across the top row, then 5-6-7-8 from right to left on the second row, and so on (see drawing below). Next, write boys and girls names into the squares. Hand the paper to a spectator and ask him to

1	2	3	4
8	7	6	5
9	10	11	12
16	15	14	13

* Martin Gardner, a most creative thinker, developed the principle behind this wonderful paper trick.

fold up the paper along the creases. (He can actually fold it any way he wants.) Here is the remarkable thing: if you cut off all four sides of the packet, and deal the 16 pieces into a row on the table, all the even-numbered pieces will be face up, and all the odd-numbered pieces face down. No matter how the paper is folded, this always works!

Keep in Mind: This trick doesn't have to be about boys and girls. You can change it to birds and fish, fruits and vegetables, or anything else you find interesting.

*The Captain's Shirt**

This is a classic piece of paper magic, in which a newspaper is folded and torn to produce a number of different shapes. The story is told of a boy who didn't know what he wanted to be when he grew up. As the story is told, it is illustrated with a newspaper, which is folded into a variety of hats, then into a boat, and finally into a shirt for a surprise finish!

Getting Ready: Open the newspaper to its full size (figure 1). Fold it in half each way, then open it out flat again. If you are performing this magic for the first time, label the four corners—A,B,C,D on both front and back of the newspaper. Then you can refer to them during the course of the trick.

Performing the Trick: Tell a story about a boy who lived by the sea. *"Once upon a time, there was a young boy who had been raised around water all his life. He daily watched the ships come in and out of the harbor. He enjoyed hearing tales of fishing and traveling across the world. The trouble was, he didn't know what he wanted to be when he grew up. There were so many great possibilities! One afternoon, he took a walk to think about the future."* As you say this, fold the top half of the paper down so it is even with the bottom half (figure 2). Then fold the upper left and upper right panels in toward the center (figure 3). Next, fold up A and B in front (4) and C and D in back (5). Now fold down the corners of A and B (6), then fold down C and D in back (7).

Put on the hat (8) as you say, *"At first he thought he might want to be a sea captain. But he thought of the rough*

---

* This trick is based on a routine by Lillian Oppenheimer.

seas, and how he hated getting carsick, and he changed his mind." Remove the hat, and bring A and C and B and D together, squeezing the hat flat (figure 9). Turn the hat sideways (10), fold flap C under A, then fold A down on top of it (11). Do the same with D and B in back. Open out the hat (12) and put it on (13).

"Next, the boy thought he might become a soldier, but he didn't want to be shot at." With those words, take off the hat and fold it flat. Fold the front layer up on the dotted line as shown by the arrow (figure 14). Turn it sideways and you'll have the fireman's hat (figure 15). Put on the hat (16) as you say, *"So he decided to become a fireman and save people from burning buildings. But then he remembered that the flames might burn him, and he was afraid of fire, so he didn't think he wanted to be a fireman."* Take off the hat and fold B up in the direction of the arrow (figure 17). Put on the hat (18) as you continue, *"He thought about becoming Robin Hood, in order to steal from the rich to give to the poor. But he was afraid he might get caught and put in jail. So he decided not to be Robin Hood."*

Take off the hat and bring the hat's ends together (figure 19). The hat will then look like the next picture (figure 20). Grasp A and C in your left hand and B and D in your right hand, and pull them in opposite directions. The newspaper will open out into a boat (figure 21).

"Just then the boy reached the water and saw a boat at sea. The boat hit a rock. The front fell off." Tear off the prow (figure 22). *"The back fell off."* Tear off the stern (figure 23). *"A bolt of lightning hit the boat, ripping away the top."* Tear off the top of the boat (figure 24). *"The ship started to sink. So that boy, who had been raised around water all*

his life, dove into the harbor, and rescued all the passengers. For his reward he was given the captain's shirt." Open the newspaper to reveal the shirt (figure 25).

Remember: The best part of this routine is that you require only one sheet of newspaper to perform it. There are no other props, the folds are simple to make, yet the whole thing comes together to create a wonderful and amusing story. Have fun with this one!

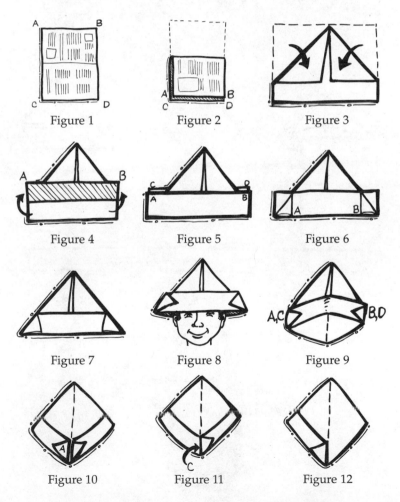

Figure 1   Figure 2   Figure 3

Figure 4   Figure 5   Figure 6

Figure 7   Figure 8   Figure 9

Figure 10   Figure 11   Figure 12

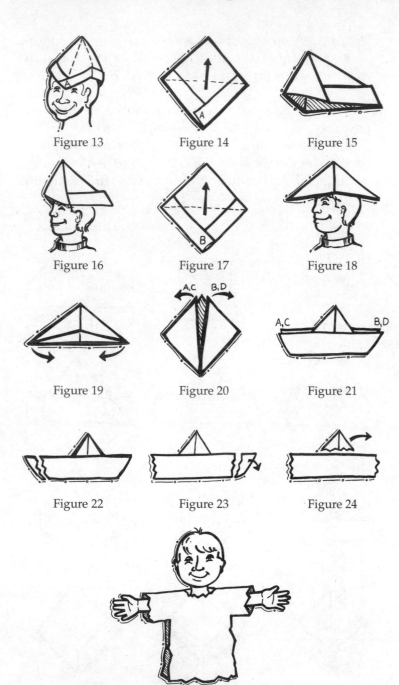

Figure 13

Figure 14

Figure 15

Figure 16

Figure 17

Figure 18

Figure 19

Figure 20

Figure 21

Figure 22

Figure 23

Figure 24

Figure 25

*The Dollar-Bill Ring**

Did you know it is possible to change a dollar bill into a ring? It isn't exactly magic, but it's a great trick!

The Secret: Begin by holding the bill with Washington's picture facing you. Fold in the upper and lower white borders (figure 1). Now fold the top half down (2), then fold the bill in half again (3). Next, turn the bill *lengthwise* and fold down the top white border of the bill (4). Then fold down the top three-quarter inch (5). This is the portion with the word "one," which will later serve as the setting in the ring. Turn the bill over (6), and fold the bottom one and a half inches up in the direction of the arrow. We will refer to this two-inch section as flap X. Fold flap X along the dotted diagonal line (7) so that the bill forms an L shape (8). Next, turn the bill around and place it against your left forefinger (9). The top section of the bill is brought around behind your forefinger and up in front, in the direction of the arrows. The result is shown in figure 10. With the bill in that position, release the portion with the "1" so that it flips up (11). Now bring flap X over to the right in the direction of the arrow, so that it looks as shown in Figure 12. Bring the portion with the setting "1" over flap X and tuck in the white margin (13). Bring flap X inside the ring and tuck it into the diagonal pocket shown (14). It should end up with the number "1" as the signet. The result is a dollar ring (15).

Keep in Mind: If you really want to impress your friends, pre-fold a dollar bill, then open it out and carry it with you. With a bit of practice you'll be able to quickly fold a dollar ring for anyone.

---

* While origami rings appear in many paper-folding books, this one was taken from *Origami: The Art of Japanese Paper Folding*.

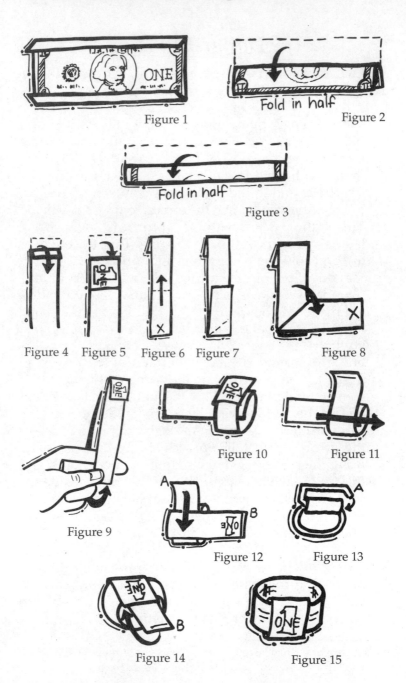

Figure 1

Figure 2

Figure 3

Figure 4 Figure 5 Figure 6 Figure 7 Figure 8

Figure 9

Figure 10

Figure 11

Figure 12 Figure 13

Figure 14 Figure 15

*Japanese Checkers**

"Do you know why a band needs a conductor?" the trick-ster asks his audience. *"Because that's what makes everyone work together. If every instrument just played whatever it wanted, it would sound awful."* As he speaks, he shows a checkerboard made from a sheet of paper, and cuts it into 12 squares. *"I once heard about a band that didn't have a con-ductor, and soon all the instruments were fighting. The trom-bones wanted to play one piece, and the trumpets another. The tubas didn't want to play at all. It got so bad the band members tore their music into pieces and threw it away."* As he says this, he drops the pieces into a paper bag. Then, reaching into the bag, he adds, *"But then a conductor showed up, and got all the pieces to play together in harmony."* As these words are spoken, the magician reaches into the bag and instantly removes all 12 squares, linked together.

You will need: one piece of 8 ½ x 11-inch paper; scissors; paper bag

The Trick: Mark off squares on a sheet of paper, as in fig-ure 1. (You may want to color the alternating squares.) Locate corners A and B so you can follow the method used to cut the paper. Fold the paper in half (figure 2), then cut along the crease from the bottom to the top, *but leave about one half inch from the top uncut* (figure 3). Turn the paper around and upside down (figure 4), and fold along the dotted line, bringing the right side over onto the left side. Then cut along the crease from the bottom up to the top, again leaving about one half inch uncut (figure 5). The upper third of the paper is

---

* This trick is based on a paper-cutting routine devised by the Japanese magician Shigeo Takagi. It, along with versions of the pre-ceding four tricks, can be found in Karl Fulves's wonderful book, *Self-Working Paper Magic*, published by Dover.

now folded down in front (figure 6), and the lower third is folded up in back (figure 7). Give the paper a one quarter turn clockwise (to the position of figure 8), and cut along the crease at the right side from the bottom toward the top, once again leaving about one half inch uncut. Turn the paper over (figure 9), and cut along the crease, once again leaving about one half inch uncut.

The Twist: With all the folding and cutting, it appears to the audience that you are cutting all the way through the paper. But if you hold onto corner A as you drop it into the bag, you can pull out the paper to show all squares connected! (figure 10)

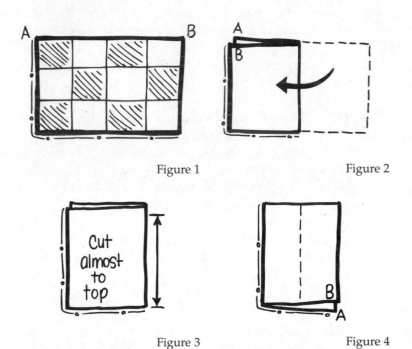

Figure 1

Figure 2

Figure 3

Figure 4

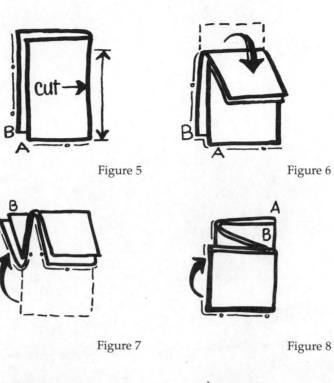

Figure 5

Figure 6

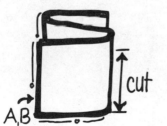

Figure 7

Figure 8

Figure 9

Figure 10

4

Table Tricks

The Secret of Success

 ———————————

You're going to learn some great tricks in this section, so make sure not to reveal how they are done. Telling the secrets of magic takes the fun out of being fooled. Remember the magician's code: *Never share the secret!*

The Anti-Gravity Breadstick

One of the best times to perform a trick is at the dinner table, after you've eaten and your family is together. It's fun, relaxing, and offers a wonderful chance to fool your parents, brothers, and sisters! This trick is usually done by a magician using a wand, but a breadstick will do!

The Trick: Pick up a breadstick and hold it in your left palm as you say, *"I was watching a movie about the space shuttle the other day. Wouldn't it be great to live without gravity?"* Turn your palm toward your body and bring your right hand up to your left wrist. Grab your wrist with your right hand, the thumb on top, the middle, ring, and pinky fingers on the bottom. *"If we lived in space, there would be no gravity to hold anything down, not even our food."* Now extend your right index finger into your left palm and hold the breadstick in place. *"Hey! This breadstick must be from outer space!"* People will think your left thumb is holding the breadstick in place, so slowly lift your left thumb in the air. The breadstick appears to stick to your hand. Shake your hand up and down, and it won't fall off. Finally, take your right hand away and grab the stick as though it were floating away.

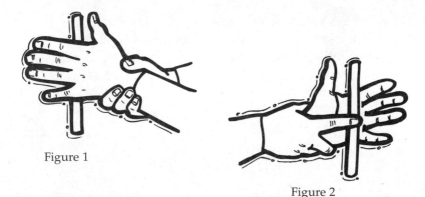

Figure 1

Figure 2

The Twist: Some people know how this is done, so here's a way to *really* fool them. Secretly slip your butter knife (never a sharp knife!) up your sleeve and under your watchband. Again pick up the breadstick and go through the same motions, but this time wedge it between the knife and your palm. This time you can take your right hand away completely, and the knife will keep the breadstick in place. Of course, you could also do this trick with a long carrot or stalk of celery—then you claim it must be "vegetables grown in outer space!"

Once in a Knifetime

If you've just done the previous trick, and are sitting at the table with a butter or dinner knife up your sleeve, here is a great follow-up trick. Rest your left arm on the table, palm down, concealing the knife, and ask for a dinner roll. As you take the roll, secretly poke a hole in the bottom with your right index finger, then place the roll in your left hand. Pinch off the top of the roll with your right fingers and exclaim, *"Mom! What did you put in these rolls?"* Then insert your right fingers into the top of the roll, reach in, grab the end of the knife, and pull it upward through the roll very slowly.

The Flying Carpet

One of the classic illusions of magic is the flying carpet—a woman is placed on a rug which then floats in the air. You can do a similar trick at your dinner table!

Here's What Happens: The trickster, hiding a toothpick in her right hand, tells of watching *Aladdin* and of being impressed by the floating carpet. *"Wouldn't it be wonderful to have a flying carpet? Why, you could just say the words and up you'd go."* As she says this, she moves the salt shaker about eight inches in front of her on the table. Holding the toothpick between her thumb and middle finger, she presses it into one of the center holes on top of the salt shaker so it is wedged firmly in the cap. The other fingers rest vertically on top. *"For example, I could command this salt shaker to 'Rise!' and it would float up in the air like this."* As she says these words, she lifts her arm straight up, lifting the shaker about three inches off the table. Her right thumb holds the toothpick against the middle finger, making it appear to float.

Remember: As you bring the shaker back gently to the table and remove your right hand, make sure you do not expose the toothpick. *"See? Floating is fun!"*

Vanishing Salt Shaker

Misdirection is the trickster's most valuable tool. By getting people to look one direction, you can do a trick another direction. By getting them to believe one thing, you can fool them with something else. This trick will keep your family talking for hours!

The Trick: Ask someone if you can borrow a nickel and say, *"I heard about a magician who could make holes appear and disappear in a table. For example, he could create a hole right here and cause the nickel to fall right through it."* Move the coin so that it rests about five inches from the edge of the table, directly in front of you, and grab a napkin. *"Of course, I can't show you the secret of how the hole is created. I'll have to cover it with something."* Grab the salt shaker and place it on top of the nickel. *"You can't see the coin, can you? You can still see the edge? Then let me cover the entire thing with this napkin."* Cover the shaker with a paper napkin, wrapping it loosely, then lift napkin and shaker straight up to show everyone the coin is still on the table. *"Do you want to watch it go?"* As you ask that question, you do two things: look people straight in the eye so that they must look at you for a moment, and bring your hand back to the edge of the table. You are apparently showing the coin again, but actually you relax the pressure of your right thumb and drop the shaker into your lap. The napkin will retain its shape, so be careful not to squeeze it as you bring it back to the center of the table and cover the coin. *"I'm going to open the hole now. Watch it pass right through."* With that, you slam your left hand down onto the napkin, squashing it flat. *"Oops! I guess I made the hole too big. The nickel didn't go through, but the shaker did!"* Reach under the table with your right hand and bring out the shaker.

Another way to finish this trick is to grab the salt shaker and pretend to remove it from an inside jacket pocket. You may want to keep a napkin in your lap, to catch the shaker when it falls, and make sure not to look down when you drop the shaker—it will give away the trick. You're using misdirection when you get your audience to watch the coin and expect you to do a trick with it. This allows you to do something else entirely. The shape of the salt shaker under the napkin also serves as misdirection, because the spectators are sure they saw it under the napkin before your hand came down on it.

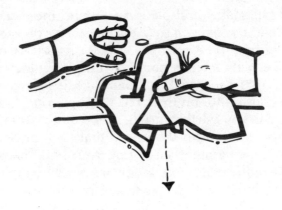

The Sheep and the Wolves

With a little imagination you can make up some great stories to go along with your tricks. For example, this is an old science project that, when told with a cute story, creates a great magic trick.

You will need: a bowl; salt and pepper; liquid soap

The Trick: The trickster says, *"Once there was a herd of beautiful white sheep grazing in a field."* Pour some water into a soup bowl or dessert dish, then sprinkle a liberal amount of salt into the water. *"Let's say this is the field, and the white salt represents the sheep."* Stir the salt a bit with the index finger of your left hand. *"But one day some black wolves came bursting into the field, threatening the sheep."* Pick up the pepper shaker and sprinkle pepper into the water to represent the wolves. *"They were just about to steal the sheep when suddenly the brave shepherd arrived and scared off those wolves."* As you say these words, dip your right index finger into the water, and the pepper magically races away to the sides of the bowl!

The Twist: To perform this trick, put some liquid soap onto your right index finger. When you dip it into the water, the soap forms an invisible film on the surface of the water that causes the pepper to slide to the side of the bowl.

The Black Spot

Select a lump of sugar and unwrap it for all to see as you state, *"In the book* Treasure Island, *the pirates mark the villain with a black spot. Somehow they were then able to figure out what he was thinking."* Remove a pencil from your pocket, and hand the sugar cube and pencil to the person on your right. Set a glass of water in front of him as you say, *"The question is, how did they do it? How did they figure it out, and how did they get the black spot on him? Imagine you were the man they were after. I'd like you to think of a number—any one that comes to mind."*

When your spectator says that he has a number in mind, tell him, *"Take the pencil and very boldly draw that number on the sugar cube. Make it as dark as you can."* Ask him to then place the cube on the table so that everyone can see it. Move the glass a bit closer to him, getting some moisture on your thumb as you state, *"Please open your right hand."*

When he does this, pick up the cube of sugar so that your thumb presses against the number, picking up the pencil lead. Hand him the sugar cube and say, *"Please take the cube and drop it into the glass of water."* As he is doing this, reach over and pick up his other hand, transferring the mark to his palm, as you say, *"With this hand cover the glass, so that no one can put anything in or take anything out."* At this point the trick is done, though no one knows it yet!

"Please watch the particles of graphite as they rise from the sugar. I won't touch you, but will merely lift my hand above yours." Do this by holding your hand a few inches above the spectator's hand. Suddenly snap your fingers dramatically and state, *"It is done! Did you feel it? The pirates have marked you with the black spot."* Move away from the spectator as you tell him, *"Open your hand!"* The imprint of the number will be very plain on the palm, and there will be a few grains of graphite floating in the water.

Here's What Happens: Graphite (pencil lead) won't stick to a sugar cube. The moisture from the glass transferred to your thumb when you moved it, and that in turn picked up the graphite from the sugar cube. When you touched his palm, it transferred from your hand to his. This is a great trick, and one people will long remember.

Remember: The use of the phrase, *"I won't touch you,"* helps fool people. When the trick is over, they will swear you did not touch him.

Silly Spoon

Introduce Harvey, your invisible six-foot rabbit. (Make sure to turn and say a few words to Harvey, so that everyone knows where he is!) Explain to your family that Harvey really is there, and he will prove it to them. Pick up a napkin, hold it between your hands, and ask Harvey to sit on your lap. After a pause, tell Harvey to pick up a spoon from the table and wave it around, to show everyone he is really there. When he does, everyone will start to laugh!

Here's What Happens: All you have to do is secretly insert the handle of a spoon into the tines of a fork. (Make sure not to bend your mom's good silverware!) Place the spoon and fork on your lap under your napkin. After you've introduced Harvey, spread the napkin between your hands and pick up the fork under cover of the napkin. As you hold up the napkin in front of you, your hand can swing the spoon into view so that it looks like it is being moved up and down by an invisible rabbit!

Fooling Your Father

Years ago a great magic writer, Walter Gibson, created a way to fool his father at the dinner table. He would set several items on the table, ask his father to mentally select one and whisper it to his mother. Somehow he could reveal the item his father had chosen.

Here's What Happens: To do this trick you must memorize the following list:

>   Cup
>   Fork
>   Plate
>   Napkin
>   Picture
>   Matchbox

Notice that the first object has three letters, the next has four, then five, six, seven, and eight. You can substitute any other object as long as it has the same number of letters. Ask your dad to think of any one of the objects. *"Don't tell me what it is, but whisper it to someone so you'll both remember."* Next, pick up a spoon and begin touching several of the objects gently, before saying, *"I'd like you to spell out, to yourself, one letter of the object you selected for each tap. When you come to the last letter of the object you selected, say 'stop.' Okay?"* Tap any two objects. On your third tap, touch the cup. With your fourth, touch the fork, and so on down the list. When your father says "stop," you will automatically be tapping the object he has mentally selected.

Quick Tricks

Salt-n-Pepper: Pour a small amount of salt onto the table, and a little pepper into the palm of your left hand. Pinch some grains of pepper from your hand and drop them onto the salt pile, then announce you can remove the pepper from the salt in three seconds. To do it, simply run a comb through your hair a few times (to pick up static electricity), and pass the comb over the pile of salt. The pepper grains will jump up into the teeth of the comb!

Separation: Pour some salt onto a business card or small piece of paper. Add an equal amount of pepper and mix the two together with your finger. Then claim that you can separate the salt from the pepper with a single twist of your wrist. All you have to do is dump the paper into a glass of water. The salt goes to the bottom, while the pepper floats on top.

Ice-cube Suspension: Give someone a piece of string and ask him to try and lift an ice cube into the air from a water glass. He'll try to do it by lassoing the ice cube, and it won't work. Then you take the string, sprinkle some salt on the string and ice cube, and wait a moment for the ice to melt. In a few seconds the ice cube will refreeze and will imbed the string, allowing you to lift it right out of the glass.

Sweet and Go: The next time you're at a restaurant, grab one of those paper packets full of sugar and say, *"Did you know that sugar causes strange reactions when combined with certain chemicals?"* Place the packet on the table directly in front of you, and reach across the table for the pepper shaker as you state, *"For example, sugar reacts to pepper."* As your right hand reaches for the pepper, your left hand covers the sugar packet and slides it toward the edge of the table, allowing it to drop to your lap. Close your left hand, pretending the sugar packet is still there, and bring it close to the pepper. If the movements are done at the same time, the movement toward the pepper shaker will draw attention away from the sugar packet. Now simply use your right hand to sprinkle some pepper onto your left fist and announce, *"Pepper causes sugar to disappear!"* Open your left hand and show it empty.

If you really want to fool people, after you have sprinkled the pepper move your right hand back toward the edge of the table. When you open your left hand everyone will be staring at it, so use that moment to gently drop the pepper shaker into your lap. That allows you to follow up your first trick by saying, *"It also causes the pepper to disappear!"* Open your right hand to show that it's empty.

5

Mathemagic

The Secret of Success

 ————————————

Keep your tricks simple. You should be able to explain any good trick in one clear sentence!

1	3	5	7	9	11	13	15
17	19	21	23	25	27	29	31
33	35	37	39	41	43	45	47
49	51	53	55	57	59	61	63

2	3	6	7	10	11	14	15
18	19	22	23	26	27	30	31
34	35	38	39	42	43	46	47
50	51	54	55	58	59	62	63

4	5	6	7	12	13	14	15
20	21	22	23	28	29	30	31
36	37	38	39	44	45	46	47
52	53	54	55	60	61	62	63

8	9	10	11	12	13	14	15
24	25	26	27	28	29	30	21
40	41	42	43	44	45	46	47
56	57	58	59	60	61	62	63

16	17	18	19	20	21	22	23
24	25	26	27	28	29	30	31
48	49	50	51	52	53	54	55
56	57	58	59	60	61	62	63

32	33	34	35	36	37	38	39
40	41	42	43	44	45	46	47
48	49	50	51	52	53	54	55
56	57	58	59	60	61	62	63

Think of a Number

It's always nice to be able to show people that not only can you do silly stunts, you can do lightning fast calculations and difficult math problems. All of the tricks in this section are extremely easy to do, but make you appear as if you have a mind like a computer! This relatively easy trick can appear to be a major mystery.

The Trick: Ask someone to think of a number no larger than 64. Hand him the six cards shown at left and say: *"Simply hand me the cards which have your number on them."* He hands you the cards, and you immediately announce the number he is thinking of.

The Twist: The secret is in the cards, though it is well concealed. When the person hands you back the cards that contain his number, simply add up the first number on each card to find the chosen number. For example, if he hands you the first, second, and fourth cards, the number he is thinking of is 1+2+8=11. Try it and you'll see: mentally select a number, see which cards it is on, and add up the first number on each card. It will match the number you thought of.

Another way to do this is to ask an adult to think of his age, then hand you the cards on which his age appears. When he hands you the cards, you can immediately announce his age.

Change in Your Pocket

The famous poet Samuel Taylor Coleridge thought this one up. Tell someone to think of any number, double it, add 8, take away half, and subtract the original number. Finally, have him add the value of the change in his pocket to this number and tell you the result. Immediately you can tell him how much change he has in his pocket!

The Secret: This trick works automatically. When the spectator announces the result of his calculations, simply *subtract 4 from it.* The number that remains is the value of the change in his pocket. For example, let's say he is thinking of the number 9. He doubles it and gets 18, adds 8 to get 26, then takes away half the number and arrives at 13. If he subtracts his original number, you get 13-9=4. Let's say he has 28 cents in change, so he adds 28+4 and tells you, "32." All you have to do is subtract 4 from the answer to determine the amount of change in his pocket. 32-4=28.

Keep in Mind: This trick can be done while you have your back turned, or while you are out of the room, or even *while you are on the phone.* Just ask the person to go through the calculations given above, and then announce to him how much change he has. Done long distance, it appears impossible.

The Human Calculator

If you can subtract a number from nine, you can give the impression of being an incredible math genius—but actually it takes almost no effort!

Getting Ready: To do this trick (and the one that follows) you must be able to create what's called a *nine complement.* The nine complement is simply whatever number that, when added to another number, makes nine. So the *nine complement* of 8 is 1 and the *nine complement* of 7 is 2. If you can keep that thought in your head, you can make yourself look like a human calculator.

Performing the Trick: Ask someone to give you a three-digit number. Let's say he names 482. Write it down on a piece of paper twice:

$$482 \qquad 482$$

Now ask him to name another three-digit number. This time he names 593. Write it under the number at the left:

$$482 \qquad 482$$
$$593$$

Finally you add another three-digit number, writing it under the number at the right, as follows:

$$482 \qquad 482$$
$$\underline{\times\ 593} \qquad \underline{\times\ 406}$$

It will look like you just took a number at random, but actually you wrote the *nine complement* of the number on the left (593). The nine complement of 5 is 4, of 9 is 0, and of 3 is 6, so beside 593 you wrote 406.

5	9	3
+ 4	+ 0	+ 6
= 9	= 9	= 9

Now you demonstrate that you can mentally perform both multiplications, in addition to adding the two products together *in less time than it takes a spectator to do it on a calculator.* While the spectator is busy multiplying 482 by 593, then 482 by 406, and then adding the two totals, you resort to the following shortcut: simply subtract 1 from 482, jot it down (481), then find the 9 complement of 481 which is 518. Write it down next to 481. Surprisingly enough, this is the sum of the two products. You'll find you can do this trick faster than the other person can push the numbers on his calculator.

Long method:	482 x 593 =	285826
	482 x 406 =	+ 195692
	Total	481518
Trick method:	482 - 1 =	481
	9 complement =	518
	answer =	481518

If this looks hard at first, trust us: *Try it!* This trick works with five, six, seven, or eight-digit numbers too, but the spectator confronted with such large numbers is likely to make a mistake. By using three-digit numbers, the spectator can obtain the correct answer quickly and the problem still looks impressive. In fact, the sum can be found as quickly as you can write the numbers down.

The Math Whiz

This trick can make you look like a total math whiz by adding five 5-digit numbers instantly. But it's easy—in fact, the spectator does all the hard work for you!

The Trick: Five different spectators each call out a five-digit number. You then explain that you are going to add them up instantly, and to emphasize how difficult the feat is, you have the spectator try it with different numbers. You write down five 5-digit numbers and ask him to try his hand at adding them up. Eventually he will struggle through to the total. Then you return to the original problem and instantly produce the correct sum.

The Twist: To do this trick, all you must do is figure out the *nine complement*, explained in the previous trick. After five spectators have written down their five-digit numbers, you create five new numbers that are the nine complements of them. For example, if the spectator gave you the number 23,618, you write 76,381 (2 plus 7, 3 plus 6, 6 plus 3, 1 plus 8, 8 plus 1). Do this for each of the five numbers the spectators wrote down. Ask the spectator to add up the column of numbers you just wrote. It will take him quite a while. Glance at your watch a couple of times, to emphasize how long it is taking him to add the numbers. Then it's your turn to add the numbers written by spectators. Do three things: *First,* write the nine complements for each of the last five digits in the spectator's answer. *Second,* subtract the first digit (the digit at the far left) from 4. Write it down at the beginning of the 5-digit number. *Third,* subtract 4 from the total. Your answer will be correct!

Magic Squares

Magic squares are one of the most interesting mathematical demonstrations. There are hundreds of ways to create them, but we've found the easiest way—and one that makes a great trick!

Here's What Happens: Draw a 25-box square on a piece of paper, and ask someone to give you any odd number. By filling in the other boxes, each row across will add up to the same total. *And* each column up and down will add to that total. *And* both the diagonals will add up to that total!

How It's Done: The only secret you have to know is *"up one box and to the right one box."* Make a sample magic square and you'll see. Draw a 25-box square, and place a "1" in the top center square. Now you simply move *up one box* and *to the right* one box, and write a "2." (Because there is no box there, we drop to the bottom of the next column.) Now go *up one box* and *to the right one box* and write a "3." Then go *up one box* and *to the right one box* and write a "4" (but because there's no square there, move to the first column on the left). Keep following this pattern. If you get to the top of a column, drop to the bottom of the next column. If you get to the right of a row, move to the first row on the left. *If the square is already filled with a number, drop down one square.* When you've filled it all in, your magic square will be complete. In this example, the sum of each column, each row, and the diagonals will add up to 65. Try it and see.

Remember: You can start with any odd number provided you place it in the center of the top row. (Even numbered squares require a different method.)

17	24	1	8	15
23	5	7	14	16
4	6	13	20	22
10	12	19	21	3
11	18	25	2	9

More and More

Sometimes you can fool people simply by asking them to do more and more quick calculations in their heads. All that work keeps them from figuring out how you did the trick. With this effect, you can determine the year a spectator was born just by asking her phone number!

The Trick: Ask a member of your audience—preferably someone you don't know—to jot down the last four digits of her telephone number. Then ask her to change the order of those same four digits any way she likes. (So if her original number was 5328, she could change it to 8253, or 3285, or any combination of the same numbers.) Have her jot the new number down, then subtract the smaller of the two numbers from the larger (for example, 8253-5328=2925). Next, ask her to add the digits in the answer together so that they total one number (2+9+2+5=18). If they total more than one digit they are to be added together again until they add up to a single digit (1+8=9). Now tell the spectator to add 1 to the number she came up with (9+1=10). Finally, ask her to add that number to the last two digits of her birthdate and tell you the answer (if she were born in 1985, it would be 10+85=95). Subtract 10 from whatever number the spectator tells you, and you will have accurately determined the year of the spectator's birth (95-10=85). She was born in 1985.

The Twist: How does it work? No matter what the spectator's telephone number is, and regardless of how she alters the order of that number, the answer at the end of the calculations will always come out to 9. So by adding 1, you have the easy job of taking a ten from her answer to find her birth year.

Lightning Seven

This little-known trick appears impossible. You ask someone to write down a giant number, then in two seconds make the chosen number divisible by 7.

Here's What Happens: Ask a spectator to jot down his telephone number, then add two more numbers. If his phone number is 123-4567, he might add 8 and 9, so now you've got the number 123456789 (don't let it end with a zero). Now, to make it harder, have him repeat that same series of numbers, so that you are now looking at 123456789123456789. Ask him his lucky number, and by changing two digits, you can immediately make this gigantic number divisible by your own lucky number: 7. Have the spectator check your work on a calculator and he'll see that you are right!

The Secret: When you get the sheet of paper from the spectator, simply erase the *second* and *eleventh* digits, replacing them each with the number 7. That's it. The new 18-digit number will be evenly divisible by 7. They won't believe you could figure it out that quickly, but when he does the division on a calculator, he'll be astonished to discover that you're right. This trick will work with any nine-digit number, as long as it doesn't end with a zero. Just make sure that whatever nine-digit number he writes, he repeats it exactly the same way twice.

Quick Tricks

It Figures: Ask a spectator to think of any number and enter it into a pocket calculator. Then ask him to multiply the number by 2, add 12, divide by 2, then subtract the original number and remember the answer. No matter what number the spectator has chosen, the answer will always be 6! (For example, if the thought-of number is 5 x 2 = 10 + 12 = 22 ÷ 2 = 11. Subtract the original number 5 and the answer is 6.)

Go Figure: You can repeat the above trick by asking the next spectator to add 14 instead of 12. That way the result will always be 7.

Magic numbers: Challenge your friends to make eight 8's total 1,000. This is not easy. Here's the solution:

$$
\begin{array}{r}
8 \\
8 \\
8 \\
88 \\
+\ 888 \\
\hline
1,000
\end{array}
$$

Calculator Craziness: Ask your friend to get a calculator and you can reveal to her all sorts of mathematical information about *farming*. For example, your old buddy MacDonald showed you how to make money by dividing the acres of land by the number of cattle. Punch in .28886 acres on the calculator, then divide it by 2.2 heads of cattle. That not only reveals how much money will be made, but shows you what old MacDonald said about it. (Turn the calculator upside down and it will spell out, "E I E I O," from the song *Old MacDonald Had a Farm!*) You can also show them what old MacDonald had covering his farm. (Multiply 203 by 35 and it will read SOIL). Then multiply the number of girls he dated (1755367) by the number of people in a marriage (2) to find the name of Old MacDonald's wife (Heloise)!

Diced: Using three dice from a board game, have a spectator roll all three, pick up any two in his fingers, add them together, then turn them over and add those numbers to his total. The sum will always be 14.

Cross Out: Ask a spectator to draw a cross connecting five dates on a calendar but not show it to you. If he adds the four outer numbers and tells your their total, you can instantly tell him the center date on the cross. Whatever total he announces, simply divide by 4 and that will be the center date.

S	M	T	W	T	F	S
		1	2	3	4	5
6	7	8	9	10	11	12
13	14	15	16	17	18	19
20	21	22	23	24	25	26
27	28	29	30			

6

Silly Stunts

The Secret of Success

When you're doing your tricks, make sure to *have fun!* And let people know you're having fun. When people see that you are having a good time, they're much more likely to enjoy your tricks.

The Magic Mouse

In this longtime favorite trick, the audience sees an illusionist place a small stuffed mouse on his palm, then is amazed when it comes alive, racing up his arms and across his hands.

Getting Ready: You'll need a small stuffed animal that looks like a mouse. Attach a black thread to it. Place the mouse on your right palm, and tie the loose end of the string to the middle button on your shirt. Now slip the mouse into a small box. Keep the box in your shirt pocket.

Performing the Trick: Tell the audience about your pet mouse, then carefully remove the box from your pocket, take out the mouse, and place it on your left palm. Warn everyone that he is nervous, then say something loud in order to "wake him up." By moving your hand away from your body, and alternating your hands, you appear to make your mouse scurry about as though alive! (In reality, he isn't moving, but the motion of your hands makes it appear as though your mouse is racing across them.)

Remember: Good tricks take time, so experiment in front of your mirror. With a little practice, you can have your mouse appear to run up your arm, forcing you to grab him and put him back in the box!

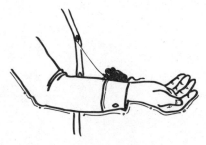

The Chair Lift

Place a chair without armrests sidewise about an inch away from a wall. Place a book on the seat, then ask a boy to stand facing the wall, bend over, lift the chair, and straighten up. It seems a simple task, but he will find it impossible to do! With his feet lined up with the chair legs and about an inch from them, he can bend over (so the top of his head is resting against the wall) and lift the chair from the floor, but he will not be able to straighten up. Next, place a second book on the chair and ask a *girl* to bend over, lift the chair, and straighten up. Even though there is increased weight on the chair due to the added book, she can do it easily.

The Secret: Most boys simply cannot bend over and pick up a chair, while most girls can do it with ease. Some people will think it is all a matter of the boy being off-balance, but it's actually a curious fact of science that most boys cannot straighten up while bent over and holding a weight, yet most girls can!

Can't Do It!

Here's a way to demonstrate something that is impossible for your friends to do, but you can do with ease.

The Trick: Ask someone to stand in a doorway so that his right arm and his right foot are against the doorjamb, then tell him to raise his left foot slowly in the air. He won't be able to do it without falling over. You can invite several people to try it. Although it looks simple, it's impossible unless you know the secret. Tell everyone you have studied the secrets of André Kole, and can levitate the left half of your body just enough to perform the demonstration.

The Twist: Unknown to your audience, you have a friend who quietly walks up to the other side of the doorway and grasps your belt. He secretly holds on while you slowly lift your left foot. The people in the room cannot see your friend, because he's hidden from view. Make sure your friend sneaks off to another room as you walk away from the doorway!

Think of a President

This trick is either a wonderful piece of mind reading, or an incredibly crazy stunt! Look at someone and say, *"Throughout history, the greatest illusionists have been able to tell people what they are thinking. For example, I'd like you to think of a famous president of the United States, and I will read your mind."* Next, you hold up the envelope, saying that inside is a picture of a president—*"the very president you are thinking about."* Ask the spectator to name the president she is thinking of. The envelope is opened and the picture removed. It is the president that the spectator named!

Here's What Happens: Obtain drawings of George Washington and Abraham Lincoln from an encyclopedia, and trace them onto separate sheets of paper. On the back of each sheet, glue a black-and-white picture of a baby (an old-fashioned photo from a magazine works well). Now put these two sheets back-to-back inside a manila envelope, and you are ready to perform the routine. Simply ask a spectator to name any president, explaining that you have a picture of the president already sealed inside the envelope. Since you asked for a "famous" president, the spectator is most likely to name either Washington or Lincoln. If she does, open the envelope and remove the appropriate picture.

Remember: You've got a way out if the spectator names somebody else (like "Teddy Roosevelt"). Simply pull out one of the pictures of the baby, announcing, *"Isn't that amazing? I present to you…Teddy Roosevelt as a baby!"*

Cut in Three

This is one of Jerry MacGregor's favorite stunts—try it on your mom!

The Trick: Tear one rectangular piece of paper almost into thirds, leaving about one-quarter inch connecting each of the pieces. Ask your mom to hold the end pieces in her hands, and by pulling her hands apart, cause the paper to tear into three separate pieces. It looks easy, but when she tries it, she will find that only *one* piece tears off. The result is the same no matter how often she tries.

The Twist: Now tell her that you can accomplish the feat by magic. Tear the other piece of paper the same way. Hold the ends between your hands. Ask your mom to grasp your wrists, to make sure you don't cheat! Now ask her to close her eyes, and when she opens them a moment later, you will be holding one piece of paper in each hand, with the third piece on the floor. You have succeeded in doing the impossible! How? When her eyes are closed, silently lean forward and grasp the center piece of the paper between your teeth. That will hold it in place, allowing you to tear away the pieces on the left and right. Let the center segment fall from your lips to the floor. (If she accuses you of switching papers, repeat it with a *signed* piece of paper!)

Everything's Backward

With nothing more than a glass of water, you can create a great silly story.

The Trick: The trickster announces, *"In Looking-Glass Land, everything is opposite. A right-handed person becomes left-handed, and a left-handed person becomes right-handed."* As you speak, draw an arrow on a small piece of cardboard, fold the cardboard in half so the arrow is showing, and stand it up on the table. *"With glasses from Looking-Glass Land, you'll find that everything changes. For example, an arrow that points to the right suddenly appears to point to the left—even though no one touched it!"* While saying this, simply place a clear glass of water in front of the cardboard. Anyone viewing the arrow through the water will be surprised to discover that it has changed directions. If you have other pieces of paper ready, you can continue the story: *"And if I write the number 08010, in Looking-Glass Land the number gets reversed. Finally, if we go in the month of May, you'll see that in Looking-Glass Land they call it the month of Yam. Everything's backward!"*

The Twist: The secret to this seemingly impossible problem is simply the fact that water reverses our view. Placing anything behind a clear glass of water will make it appear to be reversed. For best results, make sure the writing is bold and clear, and the glass is a straight-sided clear glass.

Fun Stuff

Bending Pencil: Hold a pencil loosely with thumb and first finger about an inch from one end. If you move the pencil quickly up and down, it will appear to "bend" as if it were made of rubber.

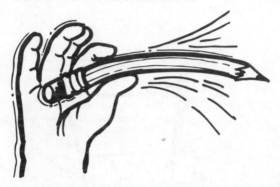

Crazy Walk: Place eight plates on the floor, about two feet apart. Blindfold a person and challenge him to walk between all the dishes, back and forth, without touching any of them with his shoes. To do so, he must not walk naturally, but must slide his feet along. After he is blindfolded, quietly remove the dishes. Then get out the video camera and tape the person sliding crazily along the floor! (After he has passed where he thinks the sixth dish is located, you can quietly place them all back!) Try this at your next party—it's a scream!

All Wet: Set a small flat dish, filled with water, on a table. Now place a piece of thread in the water, and wave your hand over it, claiming that you are going to make the thread stand on end in the water. Ask your spectators to place their heads close to the dish to witness the miracle. When they lean over, smack the water in the dish with the open palm of your hand.

The water will splash into their faces from every direction! (It might be a good idea to do this trick by an open door, so that you can make a fast getaway!)

Breaking Bread: Ask someone to hold a breadstick by each end, then fold a dollar bill lengthwise. Tell someone else to strike the breadstick in the center with the dollar bill. Nothing will happen. Announce that you've been practicing karate and you want to try it. Secretly extend your index finger into the bill. The finger will break the stick without being seen!

Delicate Balance: Ask a friend if she can balance a glass between two other glasses using nothing but a dollar bill. She won't be able to do it, but you can. Simply accordion-pleat a dollar bill, making sharp creases with each fold. Set the bill like a bridge between two glasses, and balance a third glass on top of it!

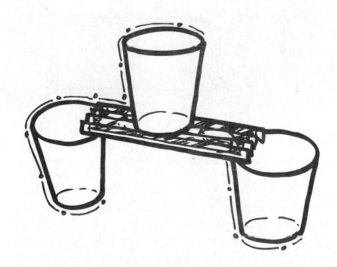

Fu Ling Yu: Tell a friend you've learned a great trick from an old Japanese trickster, Mr. Fu Ling Yu. Place a glass of water on a table, cover it with a hat, and tell him you can drink the water without touching the hat. Next, stick your head under the table and make a sound as if you are drinking water. Then pull your head up and say, *"It's gone! See for yourself."* When your friend picks up the hat to see, you pick up the glass and drink the water. You have now drunk the water without touching the hat!

Figure It Out

Match It: Arrange 15 matches as in figure 1. Ask someone to change the formation into three squares—by removing just three matches. (See figure 2 for the solution!)

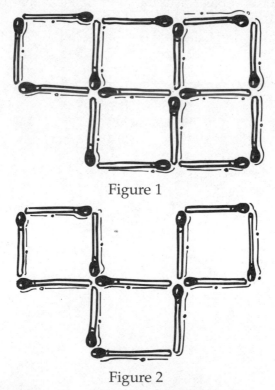

Figure 1

Figure 2

The Eight Match Stunt: Challenge someone to make three squares from eight matches. How? See figure 3—two squares are made from four matches each, and the squares overlap to make the third square.

More with Matches: Challenge someone to make *two* squares and *eight* triangles with only eight matches. How? See figure 4.

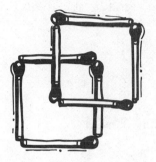

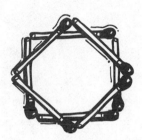

Figure 3   Figure 4

The Crying Quarter: Soak a small wad of tissue paper in water and hide it behind your right ear, then tell a friend that you can make George Washington cry by squeezing him too hard. Pick up a quarter in your left hand and rub it against your right elbow as your right hand secretly steals the wad of paper from behind your ear. Next, transfer the quarter to your right hand. At the same time hide the wet paper behind it. Ask your friend to hold out his hand, and squeeze a few drops of water onto it!

Catch the Bill: Hold a dollar bill in your left hand by one corner, letting the rest of the bill dangle. Now spread the thumb and forefinger of your right hand so that they are on both sides of the bill. If you release the bill from your left hand, you can quickly snatch it with your right. However, nobody else can do it! Try it on a friend and you'll see—if you hold the bill between your friend's thumb and forefinger, asking him to grab it as soon as you let it go, he won't be able to do it.

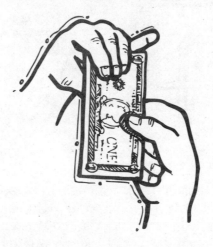

Pick Me Up: Tell everyone that you've tricked them into thinking the lightest girl in the room is made of iron. Anyone can try to pick her up—but you've instructed her ahead of time that as soon as somebody tries to lift her, she is to push him on his forehead with her forefinger. This will keep him off balance and prevent him from lifting her!

Quick Tricks

Stacked Checkers: Place six checkers one on top of another. Ask somebody to take out the bottom one without touching any of the others. When he gives up show him how to do it by placing a ruler flat on the table next to the checkers. With a quick motion strike the bottom checker. It will fly out, while the others will fall straight down as a stack! You can even repeat this until there is only one checker left.

Floating a Needle: Lay a piece of fine tissue paper on the surface of a small bowl of water. Carefully lay a needle on the paper. After a few moments the paper will become waterlogged and sink. The needle, however, will float—and continue floating for as long as it remains undisturbed!

Creating the Compass: If you rub one end of a needle against a magnet before doing the above trick, it will function as a compass. The magnetic end will point to the north!

Room for One More: Place a small, dry glass on a level surface in your kitchen, then carefully fill it all the way to the top with water (be careful not to wet the brim). Now begin dropping straight pins into the glass, point first. Even though the glass was full, it will hold two or three hundred pins without spilling a drop of water!

The Hard Way: Dip a ripe pear in water, tie a string to its stem, and hang it with a tack from the ceiling. Note where the drops of water fall and mark the spot. Then tell your parents you can cut a pear "the hard way." Carefully hold a sharp knife about six inches above the watermarked spot, with the blade up, and ask someone to cut the cord. The pear will fall straight down, strike the knife, and cut itself in half. (It can even cut itself into *quarters* if you hold a second knife at right angles to the first!)

How to Draw a Perfect Star: Most people can't draw a perfect star, but here's a way to do it every time! Cut a strip of paper about half as wide as the star you want to draw. Carefully tie the paper into a knot. Flatten the knot and draw a small dot at each point of the five-sided figure. Connect the dots and you'll have a perfect star!

The Impossible Knot: Ask a friend if he can grab both ends of a rope and tie a knot without letting go of either end. He won't be able to, but *you* can. Simply fold your arms across your chest (make sure one hand is on top and the other underneath), grasp one end of the rope in each hand, then unfold your arms. A knot will automatically form in the middle!

7

The Magic of Science

The Secret of Success

 ———————————

There are seven basic effects in magic:
- produce something from nowhere
- make something vanish
- transform something (change it into something else)
- mysteriously move something
- penetrate or break-and-restore something
- float something
- defy the principles of science

Eggs-traordinary

"You've all heard the story of Jack in the Beanstalk," the trickster begins, *"in which he visits a giant and steals a magical goose. But did you know there was a test that can be done to determine if a bird is magic or not? It's true! Take a look at these three eggs. They all came from a magic chicken."* With these words, you ask a volunteer to help you and show her three white eggs on a table, together with three glasses of water and three mailing labels marked "sink," "float," and "hover." *"I want you to choose any egg and stick the 'sink' label on it. Then decide which egg you want to float and stick that label on it. Finally, stick the 'hover' label on the third egg."* Once she has completed those instructions say, *"I want everyone here to say to themselves, 'sink.' Now watch as I drop the first egg."* Place the egg into a glass. It will sink to the bottom. *"A normal egg, right? Now I want everyone to think 'float' as I drop the second egg."* This egg floats on top of the water, as if by magic. *"Remember these eggs are from a magic chicken. The third egg is the hardest. I want half the room to think 'sink,' and the other half to think 'float.' Watch what happens."* As you drop the third egg into a glass, it hovers in the middle!

The Secret: This trick is done not with magic eggs but with magic water! To sink the first egg, fill a glass with regular tap water. To float the second egg, fill a glass with saltwater (test it beforehand to make sure—it takes quite a bit of salt, well-stirred). To make the third egg hover requires a bit of patience. Fill a glass half full of saltwater, then tilt the glass to the left and gently fill it the rest of the way with tap water. If you pour slowly, the pure water won't mix with the saltwater. Be careful not to shake them up! An egg will sink in the glass of pure water, float on top of the saltwater, and hover in the middle of the half-and-half

glass. (Be sure you don't get the glasses mixed up!)
Here is why this trick works: When you add salt to
the water and stir, the salt seems to disappear, and the
level of the water doesn't change, but you are fitting
more stuff into the same amount of space. The water
filled the space before, now the salt *and* water fill the
space. Saltwater contains more molecules than regular water. It actually weighs more than regular water
(and more than an egg), so when you drop an egg
into it, the saltwater will push the egg up and make it
float!

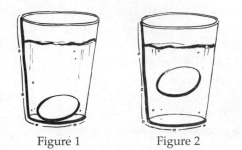

Figure 1   Figure 2   Figure 3

Stretching a Dollar

Want to see your money go farther? With this trick, a dollar bill will appear to stretch magically between your hands.

Getting Ready: Fold a dollar bill in half, crease it, then unfold it (figure 1). Fold the top quarter down to the center, and the bottom quarter up to the center, as in figure 2. Fold the bill in half, as shown in figure 3. Now cut the bill as indicated in figure 3. The first cut is made at the far left and is down from the top. The next cut is just to the right of it and up from the bottom. The next cut is down from the top, the next up from the bottom, and so on. Make the cuts as close together as possible. After cutting, open the bill out flat, get it wet, and stick it under a flat glass surface overnight. One of your mom's glass pans is perfect. In the morning, the bill will be perfectly flat, and the cuts will not be noticeable.

Performing the Trick: Tell your friends you've figured out a way to stretch your money. Remove the prepared dollar bill from your wallet and pull on the ends (figure 4), stretching it back and forth like an accordion between your hands. It makes a great impression!

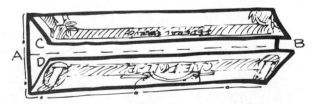

Figure 1

Figure 2

Figure 3

Figure 4

Glassical Music

"*Wow, have you noticed how many people are carrying pagers?*" the trickster asks. "*That's so that you can always reach them. In ancient times, they didn't have electronic pagers, so I'll show you what they did.*"

You will need: 2 wine glasses; pliers; thin steel wire; water

The Trick: Place the wine glasses (or any glass with a stem) about a foot apart on a table. Fill them both about one-third full with water. Using the pliers, bend the ends of the thin steel wire, a little longer than the diameter of the glass, upward and lay it over the mouth of one glass. Holding the base of the second glass with your left hand, dip your right index finger into the water to wet it slightly, and lightly begin to rub the wet finger around the rim of that glass. Eventually the glass will begin to vibrate and make a high-pitched noise. When your finger becomes dry, wet it again and continue rubbing the glass. Once you can get a loud, clear tone, the steel wire on the first glass should start to vibrate. (If it doesn't, use an eyedropper to add or take away a bit of water until you get a better vibration.) As you are doing this, tell your audience, *"Years ago, people carried with them wires like these. When somebody needed them, they'd simply rub their glass, and soon that wire would start to vibrate. That meant it was time to go home!"*

The Twist: If you've ever seen a window rattle when a plane flew overhead, you know how this trick works. When you rub the glass, you cause atoms in the glass to vibrate. These vibrating atoms collide with one another and move out, just like ripples on a pond, until they hit the second glass. The noise you hear is the same force that causes the glass to vibrate and shakes the metal wire. The only tricky part is getting the two glasses filled with exactly the same amount of water, so that they have the same "frequency."

The Floating Lady

By cooperating with some friends, you can make a girl appear to float in the air just by touching her with your fingertips!

The Trick: The trickster begins by announcing, *"By working together, men and women have been able to accomplish incredible feats. The building of the pyramids of Egypt and the Apollo rocket trips to the moon may seem like magic, but they are simply the result of many people sharing their ideas and working together. I have found that the famous 'floating lady' works the same way."* Ask a girl to stand in front of you, and have three friends stand around her. They are each to use just one finger, placing them anywhere, and try to pick her up. When they try to lift her, nothing happens. But then you say, *"The problem is that you aren't working together. Watch!"* With those words, you tell the girl in the center to stand stiff as board. You then instruct the other four to assume their positions: One person should stand behind the girl and put his index fingers under her arms. Two other friends should squat down and put their index fingers under her heels. You stand in front of the girl and place one finger under her chin. *"When I command her to float, everyone must gently lift with their fingers. One, two, three...float!"* With those words, they lift the girl into the air for a few seconds, then gently bring her back down.

The Twist: The secret to this is that the girl's weight gets distributed equally to each person. (That's why, for example, it is much easier to lift a heavy table if someone is at each corner.) By sharing the weight equally no one is lifting a great amount. But you must work together, or someone will be attempting to lift more weight than the others!

Dance of the Butterflies

One of the most beautiful tricks ever created is actually a simple science experiment.

You will need: a pencil; a jar with a cork; a funnel; tissue paper; a sheet of cork; glue; a pitcher of water; a spoon; a bowl; 10 Alka-Seltzer tablets

Getting Ready: Using a pencil, push the point through the cork to make a hole, then push the small end of a funnel through the hole. (Make sure it's a tight fit or the trick won't work!) Next, cut out four or five small butterflies from the tissue paper—the more colorful, the better. Glue a small piece of sheet cork (about 1 inch by 1/8 inch) to the body of each butterfly, to give them some strength. Use a spoon to crush about ten Alka-Seltzer tablets into a fine powder. Dump the powder into a bowl. Fill a pitcher with water, and place everything on your table.

Performing the Trick: Tell your audience, *"I have watched André Kole perform some amazing feats—sawing his assistant in half, floating himself in the air, and even causing the Statue of Liberty to disappear. But the most amazing thing he does is make objects appear to be alive!"* Pick up the tissue butterflies and say, *"When I showed him these butterflies I had made from paper, he revealed to me how I could make them come alive."* Pour the water from the pitcher into the jar until it's half full, as you tell everyone, *"André's secret is that he uses fairy dust! Oh, I'm sure you think I'm kidding, but I'm not. He even let me borrow some."* As you say these words, pour the seltzer powder into the jar. The water will begin to bubble. Quickly plug the top of the jar with the cork and funnel, pick up the butterflies, and place them

into the mouth of the funnel. They will begin to fly up into the air as you say, *"You see, it works! With fairy dust, I can make these paper butterflies come alive!"*

Remember: When you pour the powder into the water, it starts a chemical reaction. Carbon dioxide gas is released, travels through the water to the top of the jar, and out the funnel. That in turn pushes the paper butterflies up and makes them fly.

The Hands of Hercules

The Trick: The trickster stands in front of his audience, with a big person standing alongside. *"Long, long ago, Hercules discovered a secret treasure, hidden inside a cave. At the mouth of that cave stood a giant, preventing anyone from going inside."* Gesture to the large person as you continue, *"When Hercules tried to enter that cave, the giant said, 'Unless you can break the bonds of my iron fists, you cannot enter.'* So Hercules tried. He pulled and yanked, but even with his great strength was unable to separate the *giant's hands."* With these words, have your helper place one fist on top of the other and you try to pull them apart. You won't succeed. Ask others in the audience to try. Get them to flex their muscles before attempting to separate the giant's hands—they'll find it impossible. Then announce, *"But Hercules had a small child on his ship; a boy who shined shoes and washed dishes. And in watching his stronger shipmates, he quickly came up with the solution—using only two fingers!"* With those words, ask the smallest person in the audience to come forward, and whisper in her ear not to *pull* the hands apart up and down, but to use two fingers to *push* the giant's hands apart side-to-side. Though she is smallest, she will easily be able to separate the fists! *"And with that, Hercules rewarded the smallest one with the biggest portion of treasure."*

The Twist: When trying to lift your helper's hands vertically, you have to fight the force of the earth's gravity pulling down. But when you push sideways, the only force you have to fight is the friction of his hands against each other, which is easy to overcome. Even the softest blow can defeat the mightiest foe!

Glass Blowing

Tell your audience, *"I once saw a man blowing glass sculptures, and thought they were beautiful. I've never been able to do it, so instead, I've learned the secret of blowing right through a glass!"* With those words, you light a candle, place a jar between yourself and the candle, and blow. The flame immediately goes out!

The Secret: When you blow air on *your* side of the glass, you cause air to be sucked toward the *other* side of the glass. That's called the "drafting effect," and it's similar to what happens to a race car on a track. As it moves down the track, it pushes air out of the way and causes other air to rush in behind it. When you blow on the glass, you cause other air molecules around the glass to rush in and blow out the candle.

Keep In Mind: Make sure the flame is right in the center of the glass. If either the glass or the candle is too short, use a book to align them, then blow at the middle of the glass. You might need to move closer or farther away to find the perfect distance needed to blow the candle out.

8

Secret Codes

The Secret of Success

A good illusion is clear, direct, and easy to follow. Even a simple trick can appear to be a minor miracle when it is superbly done.

I Knew It Was You

You go out of the room for this trick. While you are absent, a toy gun is passed around until someone decides to be the guilty party—the murderer. He hides the gun in his pocket. Then a bunch of people put their names on a list of suspects. When you enter the room, you start asking questions, looking around at the various "suspects" trying to discern the "murderer." After just a moment, you are able to reveal the guilty party. And here's the best part: *nobody tells you anything!* Nothing is written down, everyone can move about freely, and you can even repeat the trick with a new suspect. Yet you always find the guilty party.

The Code: Your secret confederate is one of the people who handles the list of suspects. She scans the list and sees that, for example, the guilty party is the *fourth* name on the list. She then puts four fingers on the back of the pad. (Had the guilty party been second, she would have put two fingers on the back of the pad.) You can stand with your back to her, pretending to study the faces of other suspects. When you take back the pad, spot the number of fingers she has used to signal you. After you have spoken to all the suspects, look at the fourth name on the list and announce that he or she is the culprit!

Not for a Million Dollars

The Trick: This is a great mystery trick to perform at parties with a lot of guests. You are escorted from the room and the door is closed. A million dollars in play money is handed to one person who volunteers to pose as the "thief." He hides the money in his pockets, and you are escorted back into the room. You simply look into the eyes of people until you determine the guilty party. And you always arrest the right person!

The Code: Your secret confederate tips you to the guilty one by striking the same pose as the thief. In other words, if he is standing with his arms folded, your confederate stands with her arms folded. If the thief sits down and crosses his right leg over his left, your confederate does the same. She doesn't have to make a big deal of it, but can act very casual. Don't make it too obvious who you are looking at for clues, but with a few quick glances around the room, you'll see who she is imitating. It may be that two or three people are standing or sitting exactly the same way as the guilty party, so wait for the thief to shift his position, then watch to see how your confederate moves to match it. In the meantime, be moving around the room, pretending to look into people's eyes. You'll quickly locate the million dollars!

Fun-da-Mental

The Trick: At a party, place nine or ten items in a row on a table. These may include a coin, a cup, an envelope, a ruler, a pencil, a candy bar, or anything else that's handy. You look them over, turn your back, and are blindfolded. A spectator now chooses one of the objects by picking it up, showing it silently to everyone, and putting it back into place. The objects are then mixed up on the table and placed in a row. When you turn around, you can quickly reveal the selected item.

The Code: As long as one of the items is a ruler, this trick is easy as pie. Ask someone to hand you any two items as you say, *"I can always tell the selected item, because you leave your mental impression upon it."* Then ask somebody to hand you any two items. Look at them for a moment, put them down, and ask for someone else to hand you another two. When you ask your confederate to hand you two items, make sure one of them is the ruler. That way she can place her thumbnail on the number that reveals the selected item. For example, if the cup was chosen, and it is the fourth item in the row, she would have her thumbnail on the "4" as she hands you the ruler. All you have to do is make a big show of saying, *"I know exactly which item it is. You left your mental impression on…the cup!"*

The Chosen Coin

The Trick: Ask people for a penny, nickel, dime, and quarter. You go out of the room, and those inside select one of the coins as their special "chosen" coin and seal it in an envelope. The other coins can go back into people's pockets. You are then signaled to come back into the room, and as you do so, you say, *"I already know which coin was selected. It was the quarter!"* Whichever one you pick, you're always right.

The Code: Your assistant reveals the coin to you in a very sneaky way. Tell people that, to protect against anyone signaling you, no one is to say anything—not even to tell you to return. Instead, someone can wave

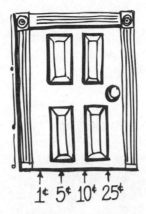

1¢ 5¢ 10¢ 25¢

a piece of paper under the door when it is time for
you to come back inside. Hand the piece of paper to
your assistant. If the chosen coin is a penny, she is to
slide the paper under the door *at the far left*. If it is a
nickel, she slides it under the door *to the left of center*.
If it is a dime, she slides it under the door *just to the
right of center*. And if the chosen coin is a quarter, she
slides it under the door *at the far right*. All you have to
do is watch where the paper comes under the door
and you know which coin was chosen. Without touching the envelope, you can wave your hands over it
and immediately reveal the selection!

The Secret Letter

You can repeat the previous trick using a different
method. In this case the spectator seals the coins in an
envelope, and your assistant addresses it to you. Just by
looking at the envelope, you can determine the coin that
was selected.

The Code: It's all in how the envelope is addressed.
When she writes your name, she starts with Mr. or
Ms. But *if she fails to place a period after that title, the coin*

chosen was the penny. Next she writes your street address, which probably contains the abbreviation St., Ave., Ln., etc. *If she fails to place a period after this abbreviation, the coin chosen was the nickel.* Next she writes your city and state. *If she fails to put a comma between them, the chosen coin was a dime.* Finally, *if she writes it all correctly, using periods and commas in the right places, the chosen coin was a quarter.* When you come into the room, insist on not touching the envelope. Instead, ask them to place it on the table, wave your hands over the top of it, and reveal the chosen coin.

A Mind for Faces

Ask people at a party to pull out four photos of friends, tell their names, and place them alphabetically on the table (For example, "Al" is first, "Doug" is second, "Steve" is third, and "Zack" is last). While your back is turned, someone chooses one of the photos by silently pointing to it. With your back still turned, ask your secret assistant to hand you a piece of paper and a pen. You then ask everyone to concentrate, and you write the name of the chosen person on the paper!

The Code: When your assistant hands you the paper, she reveals which person was chosen. If she hands you the pen with the cap *on,* it means the first photo on the left was chosen. If she takes the cap off and puts it on the opposite end before handing it to you, the second photo was chosen. If she takes the cap off and hands you the pen without any cap, the third photo was chosen. And if she says she doesn't have a pen, it means the fourth photo was chosen. (In this case, you can borrow a pen from someone else, or claim that you can discover the right person without even needing a pen!)

You don't have to limit yourself to coins and photos—you can ask your friends to choose favorite books, video tapes, toys, or anything else. And you can use the same principle for any choice of four items. For example, if you do the same trick on another occasion for the same people, make sure your assistant has a short pencil stub in one pocket, a longer pencil in another, a still longer pencil in another, and a full-size pencil in another pocket. The pencil she hands you will reveal the selection. But don't be too quick to tell everyone all your codes—that way you can still fool people who think they know how you did it.

9

Pick a Card

The Secret of Success

 ———————————

Nearly every household has a deck of playing cards in it, so it's good to know a couple of good card tricks. With a bit of practice, you can fool just about everybody with these effects.

The One-way Deck

One of the best ways to learn card tricks is to understand the principle of the "one-way deck." A one-way deck is simply a deck of cards which have an identifiable pattern on the back. For example, if the back of each card has a picture of Mickey Mouse, and you arrange all the cards so that Mickey's head is pointed toward the top of the deck, then by reversing one card you can easily identify it with a glance. One card will stand out, because Mickey will be standing on his head!

Unfortunately, most one-way decks are too obvious, particularly to anyone even vaguely aware of the principle. Some playing cards, however, are almost undetectable one-way decks. For example, if the backs of your cards have the popular "angel riding a bicycle," you'll notice that one corner has a small curl and a dot. If you line them up like that, then it's easy to spot one reversed card. You can even create your own one-way deck by using some red-backed cards and simply putting a small red dot in the upper left hand corner of each card. Most people won't notice the dot, but it will help you perform some wonderful tricks!

The Trick: In this trick, a card is selected by a spectator and returned to the deck, which is cut several times. You then take the deck and ask the spectator to think of the word "stop" when he sees his card. *"Don't say anything—just think 'stop.'"* You then begin turning the cards face-up, one at a time, and without any visible signal from him, you automatically stop the instant his selected card appears!

The Twist: Set up your deck so that the backs are all one way, then ask a spectator to select one and remember it. As he looks at it, simply reverse the rest of the deck by turning it end for end. When he sticks his card back into the middle of the deck, it will be the only one out of order. Start flipping through the cards, and when you spot the one reversed back, stop! That is the chosen card.

How Did You Know?

The Trick: Ask someone to shuffle the deck (making sure the two halves both face the same way as she does so), then cut the deck into two piles as you state, *"Often times a person's eyes will give away her thinking. When I turn my back, reach over, pull out one card from either half of the deck, and stick it into the other half."* After she does this, you turn around and pick up handfuls of cards, spread them out and show them to the spectator. Eventually you say, *"Aha! Your eyes gave it away. This is your card."* And you're right!

The Twist: When you cut the deck into two piles, turn half one way and half the other. That way, no matter which pile the spectator pulls a card from, when she sticks it in the other half, it will be reversed! All you have to do is begin picking up handfuls of cards and searching for the one card that is reversed from the others in that hand. It will be the spectator's card.

The Lazy Man's Card Trick

This wonderful effect was created by U.F. Grant, who invented hundreds of card tricks in his lifetime.

The Trick: The trickster asks someone to select a card and replace it in the deck. He announces that rather than going to the trouble of finding the card himself, he will magically cause one card in the deck to flip over and find the selected card for him. And that's exactly what happens!

The Twist: All you've got to do is find the Four of Diamonds (or any other four) and place it upside down, fourth from the bottom of the deck. Ask someone to select a card (being careful not to spread the cards too much and reveal the reversed card near the bottom). Make sure they remember their card, then have them place it on top of the deck and cut the cards. That's all there is to it! You can then announce, *"I've always liked card tricks, but I enjoy doing them the easy way. For example, if I snap my fingers, one card in the deck will flip over and tell us where your card is."* Simply spread the cards on the table until you come to the reversed card, and say, *"The Four of Diamonds. That means your card is the fourth one down from the Four of Diamonds."* Count down four cards, ask them to name their selected card, then flip it over. You'll be right!

Dumb Luck

This trick can be done with any deck of cards, at any time. The effect is wonderful, because the spectator thinks he does the trick himself.

Here's What Happens: Have a spectator shuffle a deck of cards and hand you half the deck. Then turn your back and invite him to pick any card from his half, remember it, and place it *on top* of his pile. While he is doing this, you secretly turn the bottom card and the second card from the top *face up* in your half of the deck. Now turn around, place your pile on top of his pile, and tell him to stick the deck behind his back. (Make sure no one is behind him.) Ask him to take the top card and place it on the bottom of the deck, and take the next card, turn it over, and place it anywhere in the deck. At that point he is to hand you the entire deck, and you simply spread the cards face down on the table. One card will be reversed. To confuse him more (because it actually has nothing to do with the trick) say: *"Wouldn't it be plain old dumb luck if the card you reversed, and which you stuck anyplace in the deck, would locate your selected card?"* With those words, turn over the card beneath the reversed card, and you will find his selected card.

Remember: This is a startling trick, but you've got to give clear instructions or it won't work.

Do As I Do

In this trick, a magician and a spectator each select a card from their own decks. On the count of three, each turns over his chosen card, and amazingly enough the cards are identical!

Offer someone two decks of cards as you say, *"My uncle used to do this incredible card trick, in which he used two decks. Here, I'll show you how it's done. He used to tell me, 'take either deck.'* Go ahead—take one. Then he'd say, *'shuffle* them.' Go ahead—shuffle. I'll do exactly the same thing." Make sure he is satisfied the deck is thoroughly shuffled, and say, "Okay, then he would exchange decks with me, so give me yours and you take mine." Secretly glance at the bottom card of the deck you hand him, and remember that card. "Now comes the best part. My uncle would ask me to open my deck and select one card. Do that—take your time, choose any card you want, and don't let me see it. I'll do the same." Pretend to pick a card, but just keep in mind the card you saw earlier. "Now he'd tell me to take my chosen card and stick it on top of the deck. Go ahead and do that, then cut your deck, so that it's buried somewhere in the middle. I'll do the same." You each do so, and you can even invite him to cut his cards more than once. "Now here's the part I never understood. I've selected a card from my deck and cut it into the pack, and you selected a card from your deck and cut it into the middle of your pack. Neither one of us could possibly know what card the other selected. Right?" Exchange decks as you say, "Well my uncle always did the same thing, then he would swap decks with me, and we would both look through the other guy's deck and find our chosen card." Your spectator will dig through your deck and locate his card, while you look for the bottom card you had secretly seen earlier. The card to the right of it is the one the spectator selected. This is the card you remove. "Now here's the strange part. Have you found your card? Good. Hold it face down, bring it over close to mine, and on the count of three turn it over. Ready? One, two, three!" The cards both of you turn over are identical. "See? I told you my uncle could do a great trick!"

The best tricks tell a story. So don't just fumble with your deck, tell something interesting!

10

Money Magic

The Secret of Success

 ——————

One mistake many tricksters make is that they repeat a trick for the same audience. Sooner or later, the audience figures out what's going on. Never repeat a trick. Instead, do something else that's interesting!

The Coin Fold Vanish

It's great to learn a coin trick or two, for then you are ready on a moment's notice to show someone a bit of magic. Coins and dollar bills are available everywhere, and people are universally interested in money—both earning it and spending it. The best way to learn coin magic is to begin performing some simple tricks like those described in this chapter. These tricks will acquaint you with basic ways of handling coins and bills, and will give you some strong visual effects. As you practice, make sure to display the coins or bills clearly, so they are visible to your audience.

You will need: a coin; a square piece of paper; a pencil

This is a very deceptive vanishing trick, and while it doesn't require a difficult sleight of hand, it does require a certain amount of practice. Place a coin onto a five-inch square piece of paper. Fold the bottom of the paper up to a point about one-half inch from the top. Next, fold the right side of the paper onto the back of the coin, then the left side. Finally, fold the top one-half inch down in back. The coin appears to be securely wrapped inside the paper, but unknown to the audience there is an opening at the top through which the coin can escape. Firmly press the paper over the coin, making a visible *impression* of the coin. As you handle the paper, you can turn it upside-down, allowing the coin to secretly fall into your right hand. The instant this happens, carry the paper up and away with your left hand and say, *"Keep your eyes on the coin."* Reach for a pencil, dropping the coin in your pocket at the same time. Wave the pencil over the paper, and tear the paper into pieces. The coin has vanished!

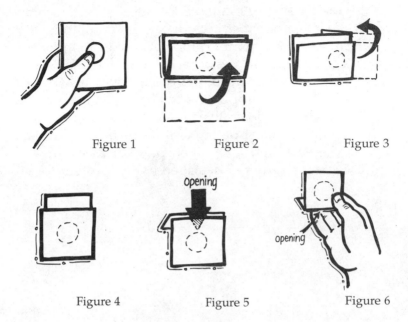

Figure 1   Figure 2   Figure 3

Figure 4   Figure 5   Figure 6

Don't just let your hands do this trick—tell a story! For example, tell people about your dog who would never stay home. *"I would put him safely into his pen each night, just like wrapping up this coin. I could look right through the chain link and see him—do you see the outline of the coin in the paper? But every morning, he'd be gone. Just like the coin! Isn't that frustrating?"*

The usual method of stealing the coin is to turn the folded paper around so that the opening is at the bottom. As you release pressure with your fingers, the coin slides out into your hand. But don't be in a hurry to show the coin gone. Let them think it's still in the paper long after it has gone, and it will really fool them. This same fold can also be used to vanish other small objects. A dollar bill can be used in place of the paper. Simply fold the bill in half so that it is more nearly square in shape, then proceed with the coin fold exactly as described above.

The Porous Coin (a variation): Borrow a nickel and wrap it in a piece of paper, secretly sliding it out into your right hand. Reach into your coat pocket and pull out a needle, leaving the coin in your pocket. With a quick word about the power of steel over nickel, push a needle right through the outline of the coin in the paper. It will look like you are pushing it right through the center of the coin! At the finish, place the needle back in your pocket, pick up the borrowed coin, and return it undamaged to the spectator.

The Guessing Game

This trick cannot be performed on all occasions, but in special circumstances it packs a big surprise.

You will need: a dime; a half dollar; a handkerchief; a watch

The Trick: Place a coin on your left palm and cover it with a handkerchief. Ask five or six different people in your audience to place his or her hand under the handkerchief and try to guess which coin is on your palm. The coin is a small one, so they will probably guess that it is either a penny or a dime. When you remove the handkerchief, it is not a small coin the audience sees, for the coin has mysteriously changed into a half-dollar!

The Twist: Before doing this trick, slide your wristwatch around so the face is against your wrist, then place a half-dollar under the watch. If the watch is large enough, the coin will be completely concealed. Next, place a dime on your hand and cover it with a handkerchief. You will also need a confederate to secretly help you with this trick. He is the last person to put his hand under the handkerchief, and he simply slides the half-dollar out from under your watch and covers the dime with it. After he does so, you say, *"Well, I'm surprised nobody got it right."* Remove the handkerchief, revealing that the small coin everyone felt is actually a half-dollar!

You can also do a coin vanish. Let your confederate steal the coin while pretending to feel it still on your hand. Just make sure the handkerchief is large and thick enough to conceal the confederate's secret work.

It's Gone

Here is a coin trick with a great story that you can perform almost anywhere.

The Trick: A spectator places a coin on your outstretched palm while you turn your head away. The coin is covered with a handkerchief, and you announce you're going to try to guess the date on the coin. *"I think it's a quarter, and it's from the year 2020!"* Then, looking surprised, you add, *"But that date doesn't exist yet. That means the coin must not exist."* Removing the handkerchief, you show the coin has vanished.

The Twist: You have to wear a watch to do this trick. Grab a corner of the handkerchief between the right first and second fingers, and as you draw it over your left palm, the coin is clipped between the thumb and first finger of your right hand. The handkerchief hides this action, and you simply slip the coin under your watch. If the coin is borrowed, reach into another pocket and grab a second coin, explaining that it has been "transported" to a new location, then return the duplicate coin to the owner.

Balancing Act

Here's one that will take practice! Ask someone if he can balance a coin *on the edge* of a dollar bill. He'll probably give up after a few tries. You then take the coin and bill from him to show how it is done.

The Secret: Fold the bill in half lengthwise, then fold it in half again. Make sure the folds are sharp. Now place the bill on the table and balance the coin on it (see the drawing). Grasp the ends of the bill and pull it out straight with a smooth, steady action. The coin will rest on the edge of the bill.

Keep in Mind: You can try this with different-sized coins to see which works best. When the bill is in the straightened position you can lift it right off the table with the coin in the balanced position!

Paying Attention

Place a quarter on your left palm, cover it with a half-dollar, and say, *"I'll bet you ten cents you can't tell me if the quarter underneath is heads or tails. As a matter of fact, if you win, you can keep the half-dollar!"* There's no way you can lose, because when the half-dollar is lifted, the coin under it has changed to a dime!

How? As you remove a handful of change from your left trouser pocket, secretly place a quarter on top of a dime and put them on your left palm. Then take a half-dollar and place it on top of the quarter, covering both coins with a handkerchief. Ask the spectator if he can guess whether the quarter is heads up or tails up. When you lift the half-dollar to see, simply lift off the quarter also, hiding it behind the half-dollar. From the spectator's point of view, a magical change has taken place—a quarter has changed into a dime.

Off the Cuff

Show a quarter in your right hand, openly place it into your left, close your fingers around it, and make it vanish. How? When you pass the coin to your left hand, accidentally drop it. Bend down to pick it up, and without looking, drop it into your pants cuff! Pretend you still have the quarter in your right hand, stand up, and pretend to transfer it to your left hand, which closes over it. After a pause, open your fingers and show that the coin has disappeared.

Puncture

In this trick, you wrap a five-dollar bill in a piece of paper, and push a pencil right through the paper and bill. You can even show it on both sides—there is no doubt the pencil has torn through the paper and the bill. With a simple wave of the hand, however, the hole in the bill is gone!

The Trick: To prepare, cut a one-half-inch long slit near the right side of a five-dollar bill (you may want to use play money!). Because of the rough nature of American bills, it can only be spotted by a careful examination. Carry the bill in your wallet and you're ready to perform.

The Twist: When asked to do a trick, pull out the five-dollar bill, keeping your thumb over the small slit. Ask for a small piece of paper and place it on top of the bill, folding the paper down over it. Make sure the bill is offset about one half inch (see the drawing). Insert the point of the pencil between the folds of the bill, but secretly work it through the slit in the bill. Poke the pencil all the way through, penetrating the center of the paper. Next, remove the pencil, and open the paper so that the spectators can see the hole. Finally, show that the bill is undamaged, and return it to your wallet. This one will bring gasps of disbelief from the spectators.

Quick Tricks

Coins and Glass: Ask someone to try and balance two pennies on the rim of a glass at the same time, using only one hand. The only way to do it is to use a fairly thick glass and rest the coins against the base (as shown in the drawing). Curl your hand around the base of the glass, and press the coins against the glass with your thumb and forefinger. Now simultaneously slide them up the sides of the glass to the rim, then tip them so they rest on the rim.

Metal Bending: Hold a half-dollar by the thumbs and forefingers, then rock the coin back and forth between your hands. If you do this in front of a mirror, you'll see that a curious illusion is produced: the coin appears to bend as if made of rubber. (If you ever do find a bent coin, keep it! After doing this little illusion, you can switch the good coin for the bent one and claim you're so strong, you just bent it.)

On the Line: Draw a line on a piece of paper. The trick is to place *three* pennies on the paper so that there will be two heads on one side of the line and two tails on the other. The solution is easy: stand one coin up on end between two others.

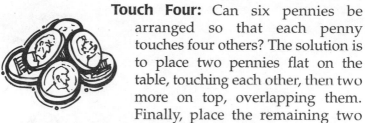

Touch Four: Can six pennies be arranged so that each penny touches four others? The solution is to place two pennies flat on the table, touching each other, then two more on top, overlapping them. Finally, place the remaining two pennies standing up and leaning against each other (see drawing). You may have to hold them in place to keep them propped up.

How Many Eyes? How many eyes are on a one-dollar bill? Most people think there are just two—the two eyes on George Washington. But remember there is an eye on top of the pyramid on the back side of the bill, and a fourth eye—the one on the eagle!

Mr. Lincoln: If a five-dollar bill is tossed in the air, what is the probability it will land with Lincoln's picture facing upwards? One hundred percent. His face appears on the front of a five-dollar bill, but it is also in the details of the Lincoln Memorial on the *back* of the bill.

Not a Half: Say to someone, *"I have two coins in my hand that total 55 cents. One of the coins is not a half-dollar. What are the two coins?"* The answer? A nickel and a half-dollar. (The nickel is the one that's *not* a half dollar!)

Can You Do It? Ask a friend if he can quickly think of 100 common words which do not contain the letters A, B, C, J, K, M, P, Q, or Z. Anyone older than six should be able to do it instantly. How? Simply count from 1 to 100!

Six Pennies: Arrange six pennies in the shape of a cross and you'll have four one way and three the other. Ask a friend to rearrange them so that you've got four both ways. It's easy—remove the penny at the bottom of the cross and place it *on top* of the penny in the middle!

Slippery Quarter: Cut a round hole the size of a dime in the center of a small piece of paper. Tell a friend you can push a *quarter* through the hole without touching the coin or tearing the paper. How? Fold the paper in half and have someone slip the quarter inside. By holding the extreme ends of the paper and raising them upward and toward each other, the quarter will slip through the hole.

How Many Ones? How many ones can be found on every one-dollar bill? The word "One" appears in eight places, the numeral "1" appears in ten more places. However, there are two more common "ones": A close look will reveal a "1" at the base of the pyramid, and any dollar printed in the 1900's has a "1" on it!

11

Tricks of the Mind

The Secret of Success

Everybody likes a good trick, but nobody likes a show-off. So enjoy yourself, but don't act like you're smarter than everyone just because you can do some tricks.

Guess the Color

Over the years, André Kole has talked with many people who claim they can "read minds." He has offered $25,000 to anyone who can read his thoughts. But the only people who have attempted are magicians, who are trying to find a way to trick André out of his money. In this chapter we will explore some tricks that make it appear you've got a super-powerful mind.

You will need: a box of crayons

The Trick: The trickster takes out a box of crayons and announces he can "see colors in his mind." Handing the box to a spectator, he says, *"When I turn around, choose any color that appeals to you. Then place that crayon into my hand behind my back."* The spectator does so, and the trickster, keeping his hands behind him, turns around to look at the audience. *"It's amazing what the mind can do,"* he announces. *"All I have to do is concentrate and the color will come to me."* Pressing an empty hand to his forehead he tells the spectator, *"Concentrate. Think of your color. Was it…blue?"* He is correct!

The Twist: When you turn around to face the audience with the crayon behind your back, rub your thumbnail across it. When you bring that hand around in front to rub your forehead as though you were concentrating, you simply glimpse at the color under your thumbnail. A quick look is all it takes!

X-Ray Vision

Ask a volunteer from the audience to blindfold you. Tell everyone how you've been training your fingers to become "extra sensitive." Despite the blindfold, you can read the serial numbers on a dollar bill, see the date on a coin, and even tell which date has been circled on a calendar—all by touching things with your fingertips!

The Secret: This doesn't take anything but a bandanna and a bit of practice. First, fold the colored bandanna as shown in the drawing. Placed flat on a table, the top corner is rolled down and the bottom corner rolled up, leaving a gap between the two rolls. When you tie it on your head, it will appear as though you can't see, but by spreading the edges apart, you can look through one layer of cloth. Then people can hand you dollar bills, calendars, and coins, and you can pretend to "read" them with your fingertips!

You don't want it to be obvious you can see through the blindfold. Reach out for things as though you really were blind, and don't hold them as though holding a book. Move them down close to your waist and pretend to be looking forward, while your eyes travel down to secretly read the material in your hands. With a bit of practice, you can fool people into thinking you've got incredibly sensitive fingers.

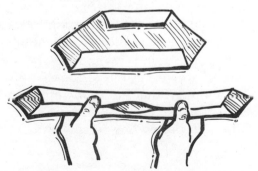

Super Memory

Some performers claim to be memory experts, resorting to tricks in order to recall extremely long numbers. One of the best ways to do this is to take a deck of cards and pretend to instantly memorize them. This may sound hard, but can be done at a moment's notice. Simply have someone shuffle a deck, then go through the cards one at a time, calling off the numbers on the cards. Ask a friend to write down the numbers as you say them. After looking at 30 or 40 cards, you can immediately stand up and repeat the entire sequence of numbers without looking!

Getting Ready: The only preparation you need to do this trick is to know your phone number and the numbers of two friends. It's easy to remember a long string of numbers—simply recite your own telephone number, then a friend's number, then another friend's number. That produces a 21-digit number! If you rattle off the three numbers one after the other, it will seem like a random list.

Performing the Trick: Have somebody shuffle the deck of cards and hand it to you. As he prepares to write down the numbers, you pick up the top card, look at it, and say the first digit in your phone number. *No matter what the cards are, you say the digits in your phone number and that of two friends.* (Make sure not to show the cards to anyone.) After you've recited three phone numbers, repeat those same numbers again. Then ask your friend to shuffle the deck (thus destroying the evidence), and look carefully at the list of numbers. At that point, the only record of the numbers is that list, and you never touch it. Instead, you stand and, pretending to concentrate, recite the phone numbers—and amaze your audience with your "super memory" ability.

Remember: There are only four of each number in a deck of cards, so pick phone numbers that don't repeat a lot of digits. Whenever there is a zero in a number, turn it into a ten. Of course, the whole key to making this trick work is to not let anyone know you are saying a telephone number, so don't make it sound like you are reciting your phone number for them. Try this—it's a real fooler!

Memor-ease

You will need: a deck of cards; a friend's phone number

The Trick: You can follow up the last trick with this one, and make it appear as though you've instantly trained a friend to have a super memory. This time take out your own deck of cards, flip them face up onto a table one at a time, while someone writes down the numbers. Gather the cards up, and ask your friend to stand and repeat the numbers without looking at the list. She will be able to immediately repeat 21 numbers!

The Twist: Set up the cards in your deck so that they form your friend's telephone number, then your own phone number, then her phone number again. Whisper into her ear, *"Look for our phone numbers."* As soon as you begin flipping through the cards, she'll figure out how the trick works. Have someone else write down the digits in order as you flip through them, and when you've gone through 21 cards, tell your friend to stand up and, without looking, recite the "memorized" cards in order.

Your friend might not understand at first, so you may want to *spread* the cards on the table, making it easy for her to see her own telephone number displayed for her. With just a quick word, you can claim to have "trained" someone from the audience how to have a super memory!

Lads and Lassies

The audience sees you write nine boys' and girls' names on a Tic-Tac-Toe grid that has been drawn on a square of paper. The names are alternated so there is a boy's name at the upper left, a girl's name next to it, then a boy's name, a girl's name, and so on. The paper is then torn into squares which are dropped into a box. Someone from the audience shakes the contents of the box to mix the names. Keeping your head turned to the side, you reach in, take a piece of paper in each hand, and hand it to a spectator. Then you guess if the paper has a girl's name or a boy's name—and you are always correct!

Here's What Happens: The secret is simple. If you followed the instructions carefully, you'll find that the girls' names all have one smooth edge. All other slips have boys' names. When you reach into the box, simply feel with your fingers. If there are two smooth

Bob	Carolyn	Steve
Barb	Terry	LaRae
Chip	Betty	Bill

edges, it came from the corner and is a boy's name. If it has no smooth edge, it came from the center and is a boy's name. Just reach in, let your fingers feel the edge, and reveal if it is a boys' or girls' name.

Remember: You don't want to give away the secret, so feel the edges while your hand is hidden inside the box. Then pull it out, keep it in your palm a moment, and reveal it after a short pause.

Quick Tricks

A Hot One: Ask to borrow seven or eight pennies from people in the audience, dump them into a hat, and shake them up. Turn your back as someone reaches in, pulls out one coin, checks the date, and shows it to those around him so there can be no question of identifying it. While your back is still turned, the coin is dropped back into the hat, and the hat is shaken to shuffle the coins before it is handed back to you. When you reach into the hat, all you've got to do is feel for the one coin that is warmer than the others. That's the coin which was chosen!

Twenty One: Hand someone three dice, turn your back, and ask him to toss them onto the table, and silently add up the total of the three dice. Next have someone else carefully pick up the dice and read the numbers on the *bottoms* of the dice, adding up these numbers. Finally, have the two people add their numbers together. Ask them what their total is, then turn over a piece of paper sitting on the table that reads "21." You have magically predicted the total of three dice! (But don't repeat this trick, or everyone will realize that the tops and bottoms of any three dice will *always* equal 21!)

Dots and Lines: Make nine dots as in figure 1. Then ask a friend to draw *four continuous straight lines* which will pass through all nine dots without lifting pencil from paper. The solution is in figure 2.

Figure 1

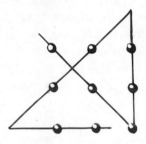

Figure 2

You Can't Lose: Tell a friend that you can place a sheet of newspaper on the floor in such a way that your toes will touch the paper, and so will his, yet he won't be able to touch you. Place the paper on the floor in a doorway and close the door, with one of you on either side!

Match Fall: Hold an ordinary book match about two feet above a table and tell a friend you predict it will fall on its side. You'll always win as long as you do one thing: Bend the match in half.

The Infamous T: Draw the letter "T" about twice the size as it is in figure 3, and cut it into four pieces. Ask your friends to make the letter T with the pieces and watch them sweat. This isn't easy to solve!

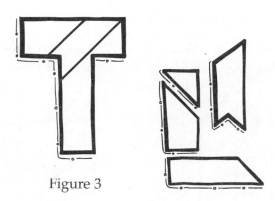

Figure 3

Mind Reader: If you've got a friend who can keep a secret, you can pretend to read minds. At a party, leave the room and ask the people inside to select any object in the room. When you return, you can tell them exactly what they selected. How? When you return, your friend begins asking you the names of objects, and you say "no" to each of them. But the first time he names something *red,* that's a signal that the next object he says will be the one they selected!

News In Hand: Tell a big, strong man (someone with big hands) that he will have a tough time squeezing a sheet of newspaper with both hands as small as you can using one hand. Give him a full double sheet of newspaper. He is to continue to squeeze and ball it up into his hand until he has the entire sheet compressed as small as possible. It sounds easy, but most big guys won't win because they try to do it too fast and grab too much paper. The way to beat them? Do it *slowly* at first, squeezing small handfuls together before going on.

Can You Draw This: Ask someone to draw the figure on the left below without crossing a line, without retracing a line, and without taking the pencil off the paper. This is tricky: follow the arrows as on the right.

12

Classic Illusions

The Secret of Success

If you want to fool people, think of yourself as an actor. It takes a good actor to pretend he doesn't know what's going to happen, or how something magical occurred. If you can learn to act surprised and excited by the tricks, your audience will enjoy them more.

Genie in the Bottle

The tricks in this chapter have been used by professional magicians for the entertainment of audiences large and small. They are classic illusions, with enjoyable story lines and wonderful effects. In this one, the trickster slips a piece of rope into a bottle, which then mysteriously clings to the rope as if by magic.

You will need: 2 feet of soft clothesline; a solid rubber ball about one-half inch in diameter; a bottle about eight inches tall. (One that you can't see through and has a tapered neck works best.)

The Trick: Place the bottle on the table, with the rope and ball hidden from view. Tell your audience, *"For centuries people believed magical illusions were performed not by sleight-of-hand, but by magical beings like spirits and genies."* Pick up the bottle with your left hand and the rope with your right, secretly hiding the ball in your right fingers. *"This bottle, for example, may have once held a magical genie—though as you can see, there appears to be no genie in it now."* As you say these words, pass the bottle to a member of the audience for examination. *"Of course, he may still be in there. You can't see him unless you believe in him."* With those words, pass the rope to a spectator on your right, keeping the ball hidden in your right fingers, and take the bottle back with your left hand. As you continue talking, move the bottle into your right hand and secretly drop the ball into it. *"I'd like to do a little experiment, showing you how the invisible genie does his work."* Take back the rope and insert about six inches of it into the neck of the bottle, then turn the bottle upside down and tap the bottom. *"The genie was always trying to escape, but he is too old to fly anymore, so he'll have to climb out. If I* *give him a shake to wake him up, you'll see him immediately grab the rope."* With the bottle upside down, gently pull on the rope, wedging the ball between the rope and the bottle neck. You can now gently let go of the bottle and watch it swing on the rope. *"Do you see? He holds onto the rope, so that it appears the bottle itself is somehow hanging from the rope! But don't worry, I'm not going to let him out. I think I'll keep the genie inside for another day."* With that, you push the rope into the bottle a bit, loosening the rubber ball, then you pull out the rope and go on to your next trick.

Remember: After you have practiced this and can get the ball in and out of the bottle well, you can elaborate on the routine by allowing members of the audience to try (and fail) to get the genie to cling to the rope.

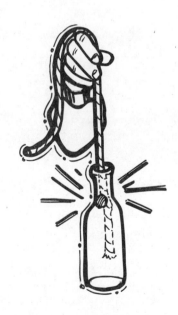

The Vanishing Wand

The magician taps a wand on the table to prove it solid, then wraps it in a piece of newspaper, taps the table again to prove the wand is still there...then suddenly tears up the newspaper and discards it. The wand has vanished!

The Secret: While the ends of the wand are solid, the middle is nothing but a piece of shiny black paper, rolled up to look like a wand. Make the wand by rolling a sheet of black paper around a small wooden dowel, carefully gluing the edges down. (You may want to secure it in place with rubber bands until the glue dries.) Slide the dowel out from inside, and cut off a couple two-inch sections for the wand ends. Paint these ends white and glue them to the ends of your black, rolled-up paper. You now have a vanishing wand. To perform, you simply rap the end against a table to show it is solid, then wrap it in a quarter sheet of newspaper, make a magical wave of your hand, and proceed to tear up the paper, wand and all!

Keep In Mind: You don't have to say anything like, "This wand is solid." Simply rap it against the table and let them draw their own conclusions.

A Wand from Nowhere

You can follow the preceding trick with the magical production of another wand.

The Trick: You display a small change purse, open it up, reach in, and pull out a full-sized wand. Though the purse is only an inch deep, the wand is almost a foot long!

The Twist: Take the change purse and cut a small slit in the bottom about one inch long. Stick the wand up your left sleeve, hidden from view. (If you need to, you can clip the end under your watchband.) After doing the vanishing wand illusion, reach into your pocket for your change purse, open it up, and slowly pull your wand through the slit in the bottom. It will appear as though you pulled the entire thing from a small purse! Close your purse, put it away, rap your wand to prove it's solid, and move on to your next illusion.

MacGregor's Cut Up

In this trick, you openly place two handkerchiefs in a paper tube so that the ends of the handkerchiefs protrude from the ends of the tube. A spectator cuts the tube in half with a pair of scissors, then both handkerchiefs are immediately withdrawn and shown to be unharmed. Jerry MacGregor has been performing this trick for more than 20 years, and audiences love it!

You will need: 2 look-alike handkerchiefs; paper; a rubber band; scissors

The Secret: Using two handkerchiefs that are the same color, place them on your table with a rubber band secretly holding them together in the middle. The rubber band should fit snugly, but not pull them tightly together. When it's time to perform, you simply hold the handkerchiefs in your right hand (figure 1), but do it so the ends of one handkerchief are sticking up and the ends of the other are sticking down (see figure 2). Use your left hand to wrap the handkerchiefs in a piece of paper folded into thirds, so that they are inside a flat paper tube. (You might want to use some tape to keep the tube from opening.) Now

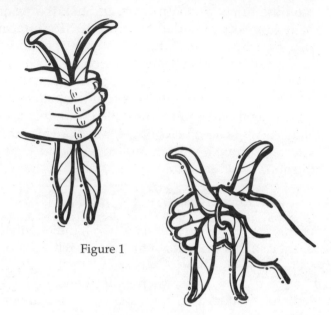

Figure 1

Figure 2

Figure 3

grasp the ends of the handkerchiefs and pull them slightly apart, pushing the tube against the palms with your little fingers to keep it in place when it is cut (figure 3). A spectator picks up scissors from the table and cuts through the center of the tube. It looks like he is cutting the handkerchiefs in half, but by pulling gently on the ends of the handkerchiefs, you pull them apart so that he cuts through the rubber band, not the handkerchiefs. After he has cut through the tube completely, bring the two halves together, gather everything in your left hand, and magically wave your right hand over the top. Then with your right fingers grab hold of any end and pull out one handkerchief, then the other, showing them to be fully restored.

Keep in Mind: This illusion can be done while telling a story, or the entire thing can be performed silently. With a bit of practice, it's a beautiful trick.

Money from Nowhere

"Everybody loves illusions, because they make it appear as though a magician can create something from nothing," the trickster says as he opens up a small brown paper sack. *"The dream of the ages is to be able to reach into the air and pluck a coin. Money from nowhere! Wouldn't that be wonderful?"* As he says this, he reaches into the air, pulls out a half-dollar from nowhere, and drops it into the paper sack. This is repeated five or six times, as the magician finds a coin behind someone's ear, under a lapel, and even behind someone's knee!

Getting Ready: This is one of the most famous tricks in history. Throughout the ages magicians have featured it. There are a number of ways to create the illusion of pulling coins from nowhere. This is the easiest: Take five or six half dollars in your left fingers, then pick up a small paper sack with that hand. If your left fingers are secretly holding the coins on the *inside* of the bag, and your thumb is on the outside, all you've got to do is gently release your fingers to let a coin slide down into the bottom of the sack.

Performing the Trick: Hide one coin in the collar of your shirt, the others in your left hand, and pick up the paper sack. As you begin to talk, reach up and act surprised as you find the first coin in your collar. Pretend to drop it in the sack, but actually hide it in your right fingers and release one coin from your left hand. You can show a spectator that you've now got one coin in the sack, then pretend to pull a coin from the spectator's ear. Once again pretend to drop the coin in the sack, actually releasing another one from your left hand. Repeat this until you've used all the coins in the left hand. Finally, pull the last coin from behind your knee, toss it in the air and catch it in the bag. It will appear as though you've magically pulled a handful of coins from nowhere!

Remember: Keep talking as you do this trick. When you pull a coin from someone's ear, mention that you've found a *"cash-ear"* (cashier). When you pull one from their lapel, say that you've discovered a *"treasure chest."* This effect can really make people laugh!

The Magic Scrapbook

You will need: a scrapbook with soft paper pages; pictures from magazines; scissors; glue

The Trick: Here is a great trick you can make for yourself. Take the photo album or scrapbook with soft paper pages (not stiff cardboard pages) and carefully cut *every other page* about one-eighth inch short (see the drawing). Paste pictures on every short page, leaving the alternating longer pages blank.

Ask your audience, *"Do you have a bunch of photographs sitting around in boxes? A lot of people take photos of their vacations, then never find the time to put them in a photo album."* Thumb through the pages of your scrapbook from front to back, revealing blank pages. *"My family had a great vacation last year. We even got to see an André Kole magic show! I took a bunch of pictures, and I think André's magic must have rubbed off. When I got home, I simply waved my camera over the top of my photo album, and the pictures instantly appeared!"* Thumb through the album from the other way, and the pages appear full of pictures!

The Twist: By cutting every other page short, something sneaky happens. If you flip quickly through the pages with your thumb from front to back, only the blank pages will show, so it will look like the scrapbook is empty. But if you flip through the pages the *other* way, only the pages with pictures show, so it looks like the pages have been magically filled! For best results, use pictures cut from a magazine—regular photographs are usually too thick.

Squash!

You will need: a small "shot" or souvenir glass; 1 foot of elastic cord; rubber ball that is slightly larger than the mouth of the glass; a nail; a large safety pin

The Trick: In this trick, you show a small glass filled with liquid, squeeze it between your hands, and suddenly it vanishes—glass and liquid! Make a hole through the ball with the nail. Thread the elastic cord through it. Pin the loose end of the cord inside your jacket between your shoulder blades, allowing the ball to hang hidden under your jacket, just above your belt (see the drawing). To perform this trick, pick up the

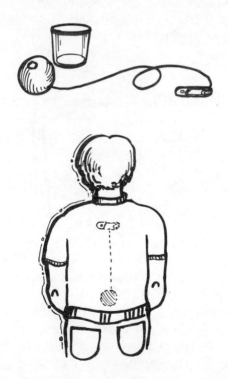

glass of liquid with your right hand, transfer it to your left palm, and turn slightly to your right. As you look at the glass, your right hand secretly reaches behind you and grabs the rubber ball. Bring your hands together, placing your right hand on top of the glass and secretly forcing the ball into the glass. The instant the ball is lodged in the glass, release the pressure on it and the whole thing will snap back under your jacket, carrying the glass of liquid with it. Your arms and jacket provide cover so the audience can't see it go. All you've got to do is slowly separate your hands and show them empty. The glass has disappeared!

Experiment in front of your mirror (without water) so that you can grab the ball and vanish the glass without anyone noticing.

Nutty Necklace

You will need: 2 identical strings of beads about 12 inches long; scissors; 2 glasses; a special paper bag that has an extra flap inside (see the drawing); a wand

The Trick: In this classic illusion, the magician shows a pearl necklace, cuts the string of pearl beads, and dumps the beads into a glass. He then pours the loose beads and string into a small paper bag, waves his magic wand, and when he reaches into the bag, he pulls out the lovely necklace—completely restored!

The Twist: Prepare the bag by following the drawings. Although the inside of the bag will appear empty, the flap will allow you to hide a duplicate string of beads inside. Show the paper bag to be empty, then hold up the string of beads and cut them with scissors as you state, *"This necklace drives me crazy. I don't like it, but I can't seem to get rid of it. I've tried throwing it away, and it always comes back. I've even tried cutting it up. Watch!"* Cut off one end, dump the beads into a glass, then pour them from glass to glass in order to prove they really are separated. Next you pour the beads into the paper bag, close it up, and wave your hands over it as you continue, *"All the beads are separate. Nothing is holding them together, but all I've got to do is wait a minute, and that nutty necklace will be right back where I started."* Tear open the bag and pull out the "restored" necklace, actually pulling out the duplicate from the secret compartment. Then crumple the bag, giving it the appearance of being empty, and you're done!

People will suspect you're doing something tricky if you say things like, *"I've got in my hands an ordinary paper bag."* So don't draw attention to the bag, simply treat it as though it were ordinary and no one will suspect anything!

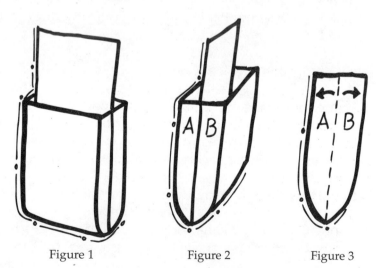

Figure 1   Figure 2   Figure 3

The Magic Show 13

The Secret of Success

A good magic show isn't just a series of unrelated tricks, but a routine of several tricks that flow from one to another. In this section, we've put together a handful of tricks that create a complete magic show you can do at home. Practice these tricks, and make sure you know what you're going to say before trying them on your family and friends.

The Birthday Party

Begin the show by announcing you were watching television when suddenly you remembered it was your mom's birthday and you had forgotten to buy her a gift! You solved the problem by rolling the day's newspaper into tubes and producing a colorful scarf from each one.

You will need: sheet of newspaper; 2 scarves; scissors; tape; paper clips; 2 glasses

Getting Ready: Cut a sheet of newspaper in half, fold each one over, roll them into wide tubes. Secure them with tape. Fold up two colorful silk handkerchiefs and place them *inside* the tubes with paper clips. Put these on a table next to a couple of drinking glasses, making sure the tubes are big enough to fit over the glasses.

Performing the Trick: Tell everyone you forgot your mom's birthday, but you noticed in the newspaper that silk scarves were on sale. *"I was just going to go to the store and buy the scarves when my mom walked into the room and saw me reading the ad. Thinking quickly, I rolled the newspaper into a couple tubes so she'd think I was doing a magic trick."* As you speak, grasp each tube with one hand, reaching your fingers inside so that they cover the silk. You can then lift each tube and hold it so the audience can see inside. Because each hand covers a scarf, the tubes will appear empty. *"But then I figured, as long as I'm a magician, I really ought to do a trick instead of going to the store."* Set each tube down over a glass. As you do, use your fingers to push the scarves down until they are free of the paper clips. The scarves will fall into the glasses, opening as they fall. *"So I just waved my hands in the air, said the*

magic words 'Happy Birthday,' and the scarves appeared!"
Lift one tube at a time to reveal a silk scarf inside each
glass.

If a scarf doesn't open up, place your left hand over
the mouth of the glass and use your right fingers to
pull it through your hand, making it appear much
bigger than at first.

Figure 1

Figure 2

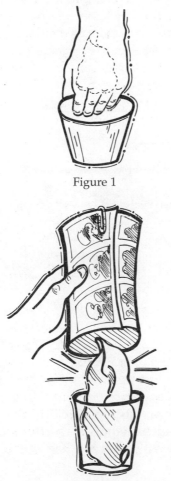

Figure 3

Paper-Bag Vanish

You will need: 2 paper grocery bags; glue; scissors; 2 scarves

The Trick: You've made something appear, so now you can follow that trick with a vanishing illusion. Take the brown paper bag, and cut out one side of it (as shown by the dotted lines in the drawing). Apply glue to three sides of the cut-out panel and stick it inside a duplicate bag. (Discard the rest of the first bag.) You've now got an extra pocket inside a paper bag. Fold it so it lies flat, and put it on a table.

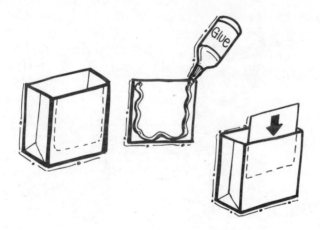

The Twist: Continue your story by saying, *"Of course, my mom looked at me and said, 'But it's not my birthday—that's next month!' Boy did I feel like a dope! So I picked up the scarves and said to her, 'Really? In that case, you won't be needing the scarves.' I stuck them into a bag, waved my hands, and they disappeared back to where they came from."* As you say those words, you pick up the bag, slide your right thumb into the pocket as you open it, snap the bag open, and with your left hand place the scarves into the secret pocket. After a wave of your hands, you can tear the bag open (as long as one hand grips the pocket and scarves firmly) showing the scarves to have disappeared.

This is a great way to vanish one or more handkerchiefs, and can be done even when you are surrounded by an audience. You'll find that silk handkerchiefs have less bulk than cotton ones, so they are better concealed in the compartment in the bag.

Hatful of Water

The next trick will change the pace of your demonstration. The props can be made up in a matter of minutes, and your audience will love it.

You will need: 2 medium-sized paper cups with a lip; scissors; hat; a pitcher of water

Here's What Happens: Take one of the paper cups and neatly cut the bottom out of it. Carefully cut off the top lip of the second cup. The bottomless cup (B) will then fit into the other cup (A), but it *looks* like a single cup. Have these on the table with a pitcher of water and you're ready to go.

Ask to borrow one of your dad's hats, and place it on the table so that the audience can see it but not see *into* it. (If they're too close, turn up the brim to block their view.) *"You're going to love this trick—it's a brand new one I just learned! I take this cup, fill it with water, then place it into the hat."* Pour just a little water into cup B, then make sure to set the cup squarely into the hat so that it stands up. *"No, wait. That's not it. The cup doesn't go into the hat, it goes on the table."* While saying this, reach in and pull up on the inside cup with your

index finger, removing the insert (cup B) and leaving the actual cup (cup A) (see drawing). Be careful that your audience doesn't see that the bottom of cup B is missing. If you lift the cup straight up and set it on the table, it won't be seen. Make sure the other cup doesn't spill and is still standing upright in the hat. *"Wait. That's still not right—let me start again. I'm sorry, this is a new trick, like I said. I think I pour the water into the cup."* At this point you apparently pour water into the hat, though you're actually pouring it into the cup hidden inside the hat. *"Oops! I think I messed up. I forgot the cup!"* Now put down the pitcher, pick up the bottomless cup, and carefully put it back into the hat, sliding it inside the cup with water. *"Don't worry, Dad, I fixed it. There's a cup in the hat. That will take care of the water."* Look into the hat and pretend something went wrong. *"Maybe I should study this one before I do it again."* With that, you reach into the hat, remove the cups as one, and pour the water back into the pitcher with a flourish. Somehow the water has been captured by the cup and not spilled into the hat. You just have to crush the cups so nobody discovers the secret! Turn the hat upright and show your audience that it is magically still dry!

This doesn't have to be done with a hat—it works just as well with a big purse or a fancy bag.

Sands of Time

This trick offers a great mystery along with a good story.

You will need: 3 drinking glasses; colored sand; cheese grater; paraffin wax; plastic tube ¾" in diameter, 1 ft. in length; mixing bowl; pitcher of water; blue food coloring; white plate

The Trick: Fill the drinking glasses with different colors of sand (colored sand is available at craft stores). Then, using the cheese grater, grate some paraffin wax onto a plate. Taking a small handful of the red sand, mix it with some paraffin shreds until you have a small sand ball that holds together. Next, do the same with some white and blue sand. Try to make the balls into slightly different shapes, so you can tell which is which just by feeling them. Paint the plastic tube to look like a magic wand. Hide the balls *inside* the tube. Fill the pitcher with water and add dark blue food coloring. Now you're ready to go.

Make sure the tube, mixing bowl, three glasses of sand, and the pitcher of blue water are on your table. Tell your audience, *"Once upon a time, when André Kole was traveling through India, he saw a beautiful crystal-blue lake."* With those words, pick up the pitcher and pour the blue water into the bowl until it's three-quarters full. *"Standing on the shore was an old man with long white hair and pale-blue eyes. He told André the lake was fed by three mighty rivers. Each river brought sand from faraway places, which mixed together to create a magic lake."* As you say these words, slowly pour the white sand into the bowl. *"The first river brought sand from a place of white mountains—the place where the old man was born."* Next pour in the red sand and say, *"The second river brought sand from a wild red desert—the place where the old man learned his tricks."* Then pour in the blue sand as you say, *"The third river brought sand from a quiet blue forest, where the old man found wisdom and peace."* Now carefully put the plastic tube into the bowl, letting the sand cakes slip into the water, and stir gently. *"Then the old man did an amazing thing. He reached into the lake and pulled out each color of sand separately. Like so!"* Reach your hand into the bowl and lift out each of the sand shapes you made, one by one. Then crush each of them with your hand and sprinkle them onto a white plate. As you sprinkle the white sand cake, say, *"The old man told André, 'This is the land in which I was born—the time of my childhood.'"* With the red sand cake, tell them, *"This is the red land of my youth—my time of learning.'"* With the blue sand cake, state, *"Finally, the old man said, 'But this last is the most important. It comes from the land of quiet blue forests.'"* As you lift each sand ball out of the water, keep your fingers spaced like a rake so any wet sand passes out of your hand into the water. Before you take your hand completely out of the water, close it around the sand ball. *"Then the old man smiled, said good-bye, and disappeared into the quiet blue lake."* You have told an interesting story, and somehow separated dry sand from wet. Now let audience members try to separate the sand!

This rather quiet trick creates a nice mood as you move toward the end of your magic show. Be quiet for a moment before starting your last trick.

The Surprise Party

To close your show, thank everyone for being such a nice audience, and tell them you have a surprise for them. Show an empty cardboard box. Say the magic word and produce cookies for everyone out of the box!

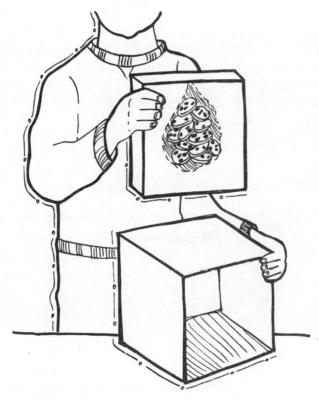

You will need: a heavy cardboard box and lid, about 10 or 12 inches square; a light color of paint; contact paper, or aluminum foil; a bag the same color as the inside of your box; cookies, a small hook

Here's What Happens: Paint the inside of the box a light color and decorate the outside with paint, contact paper, or foil. Stick the cookies inside the bag. Fasten the bag, which is the same color as the inside of your box, to a small hook in the inside back edge of the lid. Set the box upright on your table, with the lid on top. To show your box empty, raise the lid slightly and slide it forward, then show the inside of the lid, keeping the bag of cookies hidden inside the box. Drop the front down and show the top of the lid. Then, holding the lid vertically, lift the lid up as you tilt the box forward and show it empty (see the drawing). You can place the box on the table, replace the lid front first, and unhook the secret load as you do so, allowing it to drop into the box.

Wave your hand over the box, say thanks to everyone, and remove the lid to produce the cookies!

You can also use this box to produce a bunch of flowers, some colorful scarves, or even a live rabbit! This should make a great ending to your magic show!

Trick Index

Acknowledgments

The tricks on these pages come from our combined resources and a heavy reliance on a library of magic books. While there are many ideas in this book that are simply considered "classics," and we don't know whom to credit, there are at least three authors we must mention because their great books on tricks and twists inspired us.

First, the incredible Karl Fulves has created a number of excellent books, all of them published by Dover Publications. His works include *Self-Working Coin Magic, Self-Working Number Magic, Self-Working Paper Magic, Self-Working Table Magic, Self-Working Handkerchief Magic, Self-Working Mental Magic,* and *Self-Working Card Tricks.* These inexpensive paperbacks are a treasure trove of tricks, and we salute the creative mind behind them.

Second, George Schindler is a fine magical performer whose *Magic with Everyday Objects* is a wonderful beginner's guide to doing tricks at the dinner table. His book sparked several of our ideas.

A third writer to whom we owe a debt is Bill Tarr, author of *Now You See It, Now You Don't* and *101 Easy to Do Magic Tricks,* among others. His books offer great ideas and excellent effects, and the clear drawings by Frank Daniel helped us find a style for our own artist.

Finally, we want to give a big hug to our artist, Joneile Emory, who did a wonderful job of capturing the ideas in her drawings. Great work, Joneile!

Other Good Harvest House Reading

Mind Games
André Kole with Jerry MacGregor
Psychic readings, identifying unseen objects, psychic surgery—are these miracles or illusions? Drawing from his experience and study, Kole provides clear explanations for supposed miracles and wonders, and reveals the trickery behind astrology, UFOs, ghosts, and more.

Amazing Mazes for Kids
Steve and Becky Miller
Amazing Mazes for Kids has nearly 75 mazes—every single one a new and different adventure. You'll walk with the animals into Noah's Ark, fish with Peter to find the fish with the coin, and fly with the ravens who feed Elijah. Along the way, you'll discover many fascinating people and places in the Bible, including Jesus, Moses, Paul, Jerusalem, Bethlehem, and much more!

Bible Brainteasers
Bob Phillips
Stretch your gray cells with Bible anagrams, cryptograms, syllagrams, and every other "gram" you can think of. Riddles, word jumbles, and more provide personal challenge or group fun in this collection of stimulating Scripture games.

Bible Olympics
Bob Phillips
Expand your Bible knowledge with this gold-medal collection of great Bible games. Puzzles, mazes, word jumbles, riddles, and much more—everything you need for countless hours of competition and fun.

Memory Verse Games for Kids
Steve and Becky Miller
This entertaining book motivates children to memorize God's Word with lively activities, including secret code games, word searches, cryptograms, and crossword puzzles.

Squeaky Clean Jokes for Kids
Bob Phillips and Steve Russo
The authors scoured the country in their quest for this hilarious, wholesome entertainment. Suds will fly as children shower their family and friends with these squeaky-clean bits of wit, brilliant jokes, blazing puns, and clean-as-a-whistle knock-knocks.

Word Searches for Kids
Steve and Becky Miller
Kids love word-search puzzles. Add them together with the Bible and you've got a winning combination! Terrific for family time, vacations, Sunday school classes—any time kids want to have fun!